Children of Poverty

Studies and Dissertations on
the Effects of Single Parenthood,
the Feminization of Poverty,
and Homelessness

Stuart Bruchey
UNIVERSITY OF MAINE
General Editor

A Garland Series

The Use of Physicians' Services by Low-Income Children

Margo L. Rosenbach

Garland Publishing, Inc.
New York & London
1993

Library of Congress Cataloging-in-Publication Data

Rosenbach, Margo L.
    The use of physicians' services by low-income children / Margo L. Rosenbach.
        p.   cm. — (Children of poverty)
    Includes bibliographical references.
    ISBN 0-8153-1113-3 (alk. paper)
    1. Child health services—United States—Utilization. 2. Poor children—Medical
care—United States—Finance. 3. Medicaid. I. Title. II. Series.
    [DNLM: 1. Child Health Services—utilization—United States. 2. Medical
Indigence. 3. Pediatrics. 4. Physicians—utilization. 5. Poverty—United States.
WA 320 R8125u]
RJ102.R675   1993
362.1'9892'000973—dc20
DNLM/DLC
for Library of Congress   92–48901
                                                                                CIP

$N \omega ST$
$\backslash A6P3829$

Printed on acid-free, 250-year-life paper
Manufactured in the United States of America

TABLE OF CONTENTS

LIST OF TABLES

LIST OF FIGURES

PREFACE

This research provides empirical evidence of the beneficial role of Medicaid in enhancing access to health care among low-income children. Compared with low-income children who were privately insured or uninsured, those on Medicaid actually had a higher likelihood of seeing a private physician. Moreover, the number of visits by Medicaid children was higher than those by uninsured children. The results of this research have been used to justify Congressionally-mandated expansions of Medicaid eligibility to low-income children who would otherwise not have been covered by Medicaid because they do not meet their state's categorical or financial eligibility criteria.

Yet, despite expansions of Medicaid eligibility, low-income children are still disproportionately represented among the uninsured. Rising health insurance costs have forced many employers to eliminate coverage of dependents, impose employee cost-sharing, or drop coverage altogether, leaving many families without even basic health care coverage. Children in near poor families would not be eligible for Medicaid unless they encounter catastrophic medical expenses and qualify as medically needy by "spending down" onto Medicaid.

Thus, the results of this study are still timely, despite the time that has elapsed since the study was conducted (1985) or the data were collected (1980). As the public outcry for national health reform mounts, this study may contribute to the debate by shedding light on the value of Medicaid coverage in stimulating the use of health services by low-income children, and shifting the locus of care from more expensive to less expensive settings.

While conducting this research in 1984-1985, I received support and encouragement from many individuals. I would like to acknowledge the invaluable contributions of my dissertation committee: Stanley Wallack (chair), Lorraine Klerman, Mary Grace Kovar, and Norman Kurtz. I appreciate their continued support as I pursue my career in health policy research.

Financial assistance for this research was provided by the National Center for Health Services Research (Grant No. HS 05230), Jon Gabel, Project Officer. Additional in-kind assistance, including office space, computer access, and technical assistance was provided by the National Center for Health Statistics, Utilization and Expenditure Branch. I am especially indebted to Mary Grace Kovar, Bob Wright and Michele Chyba for their support.

The manuscript was prepared for publication by Cheryl Englehart, Executive Assistant, Center for Health Economics Research. Her attention to detail, her precision in typing, and her good humor made the task of revisiting the dissertation all the more pleasant. Killard Adamache, Carol

Ammering, and Linda DeMarco contributed invaluable assistance in producing the manuscript.

Last but not least, I would like to acknowledge my family and friends who not only supported me during the dissertation phase, but have continued to support me during my career at Center for Health Economics Research: Carolyn and Elias Gottlieb, David Lambert, Thomas McGuire, and Joan and Hans Rosenbach. To my daughter, Dana Rose Gottlieb, you have taught me the joys of parenthood. And to my husband, Robert Gottlieb, none of this would have been possible without your support, understanding, and sacrifice.

The views and opinions expressed herein are my own and any errors of omission or comission are my sole responsibility.

Margo L. Rosenbach
Center for Health Economics
Research

The Use of Physicians' Services by Low-Income Children

Chapter 1

INTRODUCTION AND OVERVIEW

Two arguments have dominated political debate in support of public financing of child health programs. The first centers around a commitment to the intrinsic value of childhood, regardless of the long-run payoffs to be accrued. Child health services, it is argued, will enhance the quality of childhood over the short-term. The second argument justifies public funding for child health services as an investment, over the long-term, in a major economic asset. Healthy children are considered a valuable resource as future producers in the national economy.

These two arguments have been the basis for an active federal role in financing health programs for children. Since the mid-1960s, Congress and the federal government have pursued a two-pronged strategy to promote the health of mothers and children in the United States.[1] They have sought to stimulate the *supply* of health services through a variety of formula, project, and manpower support grants, targeted at rural and low-income communities that were identified as "under-doctored" and hence, underserved.[2] Children were to be among the major beneficiaries of these primary care initiatives.

Policy-makers have also sought to increase the *demand* for services by reducing financial barriers to health care. Thus, the Medicaid program (Title XIX of the Social Security Act) was enacted in 1965. Children under age 21 comprise the single largest Medicaid beneficiary group--50 percent of the recipients in fiscal year 1980 (Sawyer, et al. 1983).[3] An explicit goal of the Medicaid program was to enable the poor to obtain medical care from the private sector. Stevens and Stevens (1974) comment:

> . . . the 1965 legislation promised to extend the concept of vendor payments . . . to a system much more like that of private insurance. Indeed, there was considerable discussion at the time of Medicaid's passage emphasizing that the poor would receive the same care, from the same sources, as the

rich: this was knows as bringing Medicaid recipients into the "mainstream" of medicine.

Following an extensive review of federal health programs, the Select Panel for the Promotion of Child Health (1981) reported, "There is a widespread but erroneous assumption...that Medicaid has guaranteed the poor access to health care." In 1982, about one-fourth of the children in poverty did not receive Medicaid (Children's Defense Fund, 1984a).[4] An oft-mentioned strategy for improving the insurance status of low-income children is to reduce the variation among states in categorical and financial eligibility criteria for Medicaid.

In June 1984, Congress passed the Child Health Assurance Program (CHAP) to expand Medicaid coverage to pregnant women, infants, and children under age 5 who are living below each state's poverty standard but who are uninsured. CHAP was enacted as part of the Deficit Reduction Act of 1984 (Public Law 98-369). The Children's Defense Fund (1984b) estimates that as many as 400,000 children in 25 states will receive Medicaid coverage as a result of CHAP. The implicit logic is that the expanded Medicaid coverage would provide increased access to health services. However, only weak evidence was presented in testimony on behalf of CHAP that Medicaid coverage increases access to child health services.[5]

Several questions concerning the potential effect of CHAP may be posed:

- What are the levels of utilization for children on Medicaid versus those not on Medicaid?

- Are there any unintended consequences of Medicaid coverage particularly related to the source of care?

- What is the effect of Medicaid relative to other factors in determining who uses physicians' services and how much?

- Are there other intervention strategies that might be more effective in influencing physician use?

Whether Medicaid coverage actually increases the use of health services is an empirical question. This study was formulated as a result of a perceived gap in the literature concerning the effect of Medicaid and other factors on the use of physicians' services by low-income children. The next section examines the concept of "access" as it is generally applied to health care. The following two sections review and evaluate the literature pertaining to Medicaid and physician use.

THE CONCEPT OF ACCESS IN HEALTH CARE

Two broad measures of access have typically been employed in research concerning health service use. First, "process" indicators reflect characteristics of the delivery system (e.g., physicians per population, waiting time, travel time). Second, "outcome" indicators portray an individual's entry into and journey through the health care system, as measured by various utilization rates (Aday and Andersen, 1975). In Andersen and Newman's (1973) terms, the first definition represents "potential" access, while the latter more directly measures "realized" access.

The President's Commission for the Study of Ethical Problems in Medicine and Biomedical and Behavioral Research (1983) raised the issue of what connotes "equitable" access. Their definition incorporates aspects of both "realized" and "potential" access. Concerning the "appropriate" level of care--realized access--the Commission rejected the notions that (1) an equal level of care should be available to all (given varying tastes and preferences): and (2) individuals should receive as much care as they need or can benefit from (given limited resources). Instead, equitable access is defined as "enough care to achieve sufficient welfare, opportunity, information, and evidence of interpersonal concern to facilitate a reasonably full and satisfying life. That level can be termed 'an adequate level of health care.'"

The Commission points out two major strengths of this concept. First, it does not generate an open-ended obligation. Additionally, it allows individuals to exceed an adequate level of care (subject to an income constraint), which may be unequal, but not inequitable, by definition.

The Commission concluded that a definition of equitable access should also take into account the burden involved in obtaining care--potential access--including the direct money costs associated with the care, and such indirect costs as waiting and travel time, and availability of transportation. While discrepancies among groups would not necessarily signify inequitable access, they might suggest that some individuals face excessive burdens in obtaining care. At the extreme, they might be an indicator of racial or ethnic discrimination.

Most of the studies reviewed in the next section employ various measures of "realized" access, such as probability of a physician visit, likelihood of a preventive exam, or number of physician visits. A few studies examine the effect of Medicaid on the type of regular source of care, a measure of "potential" access.

EFFECT OF MEDICAID ON
PHYSICIAN USE BY LOW-INCOME CHILDREN

It seems clear that the federal government's combined demand/supply strategy has increased the utilization of physicians' services by low-income children. Whereas in 1964, 33 percent of the poor children and 15 percent of the nonpoor children had no physician contact in the previous two years, by 1978 the figures had decreased to 13 percent (poor) and 10 percent (nonpoor). The differential in average number of physician visits was also narrowed: average use by poor children increased from 2.3 contacts in 1964 to 4.0 contacts in 1978; nonpoor children went from 4.0 contacts to 4.2 contacts (Madans and Kleinman, 1981).[6]

These data should be interpreted with caution. Not all of this large increase in physician use can be attributed to the Medicaid program, because of concurrent efforts to stimulate the supply of services in low-income areas.[7] Another caveat has been expressed by Wilensky and Berk (1982). They advise that it is misleading and inaccurate to assume that the low-income population is synonomous with the Medicaid population. With data from the 1977 National Medical Care Expenditure Survey (NMCES), they traced the insurance status of poor and near poor children (less than 125 percent of poverty) over the course of the year. They estimated that 48 percent of the low-income children had Medicaid coverage for at least part of the year; 39 percent had private insurance for all or part of the year; and 13 percent were uninsured for the entire year.

Previous research related to the effect of Medicaid on pediatric utilization is suggestive (but not conclusive) that Medicaid improves access to health care among low-income children, while simultaneously limiting their access to private physicians. Gortmaker (1981) estimated the effect of Medicaid on the health care utilization of children in Flint, Michigan in 1977. Compared to non-Medicaid children (all incomes), the Medicaid children had a significantly higher probability of a physician visit within the last year, although there was no difference in the mean number of illness-related visits. However, the Medicaid children were less likely to have a physician for a regular source of care. According to Gortmaker, this is evidence of the "continued existence of (a) 'two-tiered' system of health care."

Colle and Grossman (1978) support Gortmaker's mixed review of the effect of Medicaid on pediatric utilization. Based on a national sample of preschool children, Colle and Grossman found that Medicaid had a positive effect on the probabilities of physician contact and of a preventive checkup but was negatively associated with the number of visits to office-based physicians, particularly specialists.

Ongoing child health surveys conducted in Rochester, New York provide additional evidence of the impact of Medicaid on a child's regular source of care. In 1967-1968, shortly after the enactment of Medicaid, most (75 percent) Medicaid-eligible families anticipated that they would not change their source of care, nor did they expect to increase their use of medical care (Tryon, Powell, and Roghmann, 1970). In fact, nine months after the implementation of Medicaid, Roghmann, Haggerty, and Lorenz (1971) concluded that the pattern of care had not changed dramatically. However, a later survey documented a substantial shift in the regular source of care (Roghmann, 1975). From 1967 to 1971, the percent of children with a regular physician decreased from 45 percent to 28 percent, while the percent with a regular place increased from 33 percent to 57 percent. In addition, the percent with no regular source decreased from 27 percent to 15 percent. However, these shifts were accompanied by the expansion of public health clinics and the establishment of a neighborhood health center. A multivariate analysis of the percent of visits to specific providers confirmed these earlier findings. Controlling for a wide range of factors associated with utilization, Wolfe (1980) found that children on Medicaid were less likely to visit private physicians and more likely to use health centers and clinics in Rochester, New York.

Okada and Wan (1980) studied the impact of community health centers (CHCs) and Medicaid on health service use in five low-income communities.[8] Based on an initial survey from 1968 to 1971 and a followup survey from 1975, they found that CHC users had a higher rate of physician visits than those using other sources of care. Medicaid recipients had higher physician use than those who were privately insured or uninsured, regardless of the usual source of care. Overall, the average number of physician visits among children under age 17 increased in the five areas from 2.5 visits (1968-1971) to 2.7 visits (1975).

Other selected studies of Medicaid and physician use are worth reviewing, although they did not focus specifically on children. Gold (1984) analyzed the demand for outpatient hospital care using the health service area as the unit of analysis. She replicated an earlier study by Davis and Russell (1972) and confirmed that Medicaid coverage was positively associated with demand for outpatient hospital care. In an extension of the earlier study, she found that demand for outpatient hospital care was reduced in states with higher Medicaid reimbursement for physicians (relative to Medicare). Thus, Medicaid recipients in states with relatively generous physician payment levels were more likely to seek and obtain office-based care. Gold noted, "Medicaid coverage heightens demand for outpatient services, but...this demand is reduced to the extent that the state Medicaid program reimburses more adequately for office-based physician care."

Several studies based on the 1977 National Medical Care Expenditure Survey provide additional evidence on the effect of insurance (including Medicaid) on ambulatory care use. Wilensky, Walden, and Kasper (1981) found that children (all incomes) who were insured the entire year had, on average, more visits than those who were uninsured the full year. Those insured only part of the year fell in between these two groups. However, the "part year insured" children were found to have higher use during the insured period than the uninsured period. Furthermore, use during the insured period was higher than use by those who were insured the entire year.[9] Concerning the health status of the "part year insured" children, Wilensky and Walden (1981) found that their level of disability was as high during the uninsured period as the insured period, although their health service use while uninsured was considerably lower.

Another NMCES study focused on the relationship between insurance and health service use by the poor and near poor population (Wilensky and Berk, 1982). Comparing physician use by children (all incomes) who were sick, the authors found that the always uninsured had less than half the number of physician visits than those on Medicaid the entire year. They concluded that Medicaid has had a major effect on health service use by the poor, but the uninsured (particularly those who are sick) are of "great concern."

EVALUATION OF PREVIOUS RESEARCH

It is hypothesized the both the descriptive and multivariate analyses have underestimated the effect of Medicaid on the use of physician's services by low-income children. Descriptive data clearly indicate that low-income children have experienced an increase in physician contacts since the implementation of Medicaid. However, given the sizable proportion of poor children not on Medicaid, aggregate data on the low-income population may mask the utilization differences between those on Medicaid and those not on Medicaid.

Multivariate analyses (principally those by Colle and Grossman, Gortmaker, and Wolfe) also may have underestimated the effect of Medicaid on physician utilization. These studies have included children of all socioeconomic levels, rather than focusing on low-income children. Clearly studies of the general population are invaluable in comparing the utilization patterns of Medicaid children versus those who are privately insured. However, an analysis of low-income children may be preferable for evaluating alternative health policies that are targeted toward the low-income rather than the general population. For instance, Holahan (1975) questions whether estimates of price and income sensitivity will vary when based on the general population versus the low-income population.

Previous research is limited in several other respects. First, most studies were based on state or local interview surveys, precluding generalizability of the findings to the national level.[10] A second limitation concerns the age group of the sample. Colle and Grossman studied preschoolers (ages 1 to 5); Wolfe's sample was between ages 1 and 11. Most studies excluded adolescents, a group that tends to fall through the cracks in the health care system.

The three most relevant studies were based on data from the 1970s. Colle and Grossman used data collected in 1970; Wolfe's data were from 1975; and Gortmaker's from 1977. Changes in the "market" for physicians' services (both in terms of supply-side an demand-side characteristics) most likely have occurred since 1970, potentially affecting the relative importance of the determinants of physician utilization among low-income children. This is especially salient in the case of the Medicaid program, due to changes in eligibility and benefits.

Finally, some of the studies suffer from inadequate statistical controls. Simplistic comparisons between two population groups are insufficient for determining whether significant differences in utilization patterns exist. Multivariate models are required to adjust for factors that are known to affect use. For example, Gortmaker did not adequately control for other variables before making some comparisons between Medicaid and non-Medicaid children.

STUDY OVERVIEW

This study is designed to evaluate (through statistical techniques) the determinants of physician utilization among low-income children. Special emphasis is given to the effect of Medicaid coverage on the probability and volume of use, as well as on the place of visit (physician visits in any setting versus those in a physician's office). Data for this study are from the 1980 National Medical Care Utilization and Expenditure Survey (NMCUES). The sample for this study is restricted to children under age 18 in families with incomes below 150 percent of the federal poverty level in 1980.

The analysis is carried out in three phases: (1) developing a profile of the low-income children on Medicaid versus those not on Medicaid, with respect to socioeconomic characteristics and utilization patterns; (2) assessing the relative importance of a variety of factors on multiple indices of utilization, particularly the independent effect of Medicaid once other variables are controlled; and (3) deriving predicated utilization measures (controlling for factors known to affect use), according to health status and Medicaid coverage.

These analyses are designed to provide two pieces of information concerning the effect of Medicaid on physician use. First, the research findings may assist policy-makers in assessing the potential effectiveness of alternate strategies to influence physician use among low-income children. Second, the analysis of predicated utilization by Medicaid and non-Medicaid low-income children should inform policy-makers, in an easily interpretable format, of the magnitude and direction of utilization differences between the two groups during 1980. Specifically, claims that Medicaid increases the quantity of visits while reducing the likelihood of an office-based visit are investigated.

OUTLINE OF THE DISSERTATION

The next chapter discusses theoretical perspectives and empirical findings from previous research on factors associated with pediatric utilization. Chapter 3 describes the design for this study, including the list of research questions; an overview of the data set; criteria for sample selection; specification of the dependent variables; operationalization of the independent variables; and implications of the complex survey design. Chapter 4 presents the findings from the descriptive analysis of Medicaid and non-Medicaid children, including their socioeconomic characteristics and utilization patterns. The results of the regression analysis are discussed in Chapter 5, along with estimates of predicted utilization rates for the Medicaid and non-Medicaid children. The final chapter discusses the policy implications of the study.

NOTES

1. Prior to the mid-1960s, federal funds were provided to state maternal and child health agencies through formula grants authorized under Title V of the Social Security Act. These funds have been provided since 1935.

2. These supply-based initiatives have included: (1) formula grants to state health agencies under the Title V Maternal and Child Health program; (2) project grants (under Title V) in support of local projects for maternity and infant care, medical care for children and youth, family planning, dental health care for children, and intensive infant care; (3) project grants for the development and operation of community health centers; (4) manpower education grants for expanded training of health professionals; and (5) assignment of medical/dental personnel to underserved areas through the National Health Service Corps program.

3. Unpublished data from the U.S. Department of Health and Human Services indicate that Medicaid covered 10.7 million medically and categorically needy children (under age 21) in 1980, compared to 11.4 million in 1975 and 10.9 million in 1983. Average expenditures per child (federal and state combined) rose from $238 in 1975 to $355 in 1980 to $415 in 1983. This represents an increase of 49 percent from 1975 to 1980, and 17 percent from 1980 to 1983. By comparison, the Consumer Price Index for medical care rose at a faster pace during these two time periods; 58 percent (1975-1980) and 33 percent (1980-1983) (U.S. Department of Commerce, 1983).

4. According to Kovar and Meny (1981), within individual states the proportion of poor children covered by Medicaid ranged from 20 percent to 72 percent in 1980.

5. See, for example, testimony presented by Davis or by Weitz before the Subcommittee on Health and the Environment, Committee on Energy and Commerce, U.S. House of Representatives, July 15, 1983 (U.S. Congress, 1983).

6. Physician contacts include both face-to-face visits and telephone calls (excluding calls for appointments).

7. Altman (1983) summarizes this general phenomenon as follows:

> While it is impossible to establish precisely the
> extent to which government programs were

responsible for these gains in access to health services--clearly other factors, including a substantial increase in physician supply, were involved--there are ample data to suggest that Medicaid and other government programs have made a major contribution with regard to access to care.

8. The five low-income communities were: Southside Atlanta, Georgia; Peninsula Charleston, South Carolina; Roxbury, Massachusetts; Wayne Miner, Kansas City, Missouri; and East Palo Alto, California.

9. The following data supplement the text discussion on health service use according to insurance status. The data are for children of all incomes, under age 6 and ages 6 to 17, and are adapted from Wilensky, Walden, and Kasper (1981).

Insurance Coverage	Under Age 6	Ages 6 to 17
Always insured	4.3	2.7
Always uninsured	2.7	1.5
Insured some of the time	4.1	2.2
When insured	7.6	2.8
When uninsured	3.9	1.9

10. An alternate view was expressed by Okada and Wan (1980):

"...national data often do not accurately reflect local situations and, in fact, they often average out variations across local areas."

This concern can be alleviated through multivariate analyses that adequately "control" for local situations.

Chapter 2

DETERMINANTS OF PHYSICIAN USE BY CHILDREN: A REVIEW OF THE LITERATURE

Research on the utilization of child health services has advanced from analyses of simplistic bivariate relationships to the specification of complex multivariate models. Early research looked at care-seeking patterns of families, as well as the effect of experimental programs--such as neighborhood health centers, children and youth clinics, or prepaid group practices--on overall use of services and frequently on the use of hospital-based services.[1] These studies used frequency distributions, crosstabulations, and occasionally tests of significance (e.g., chi-square, t-test) to describe and compare users and non-users.

More recently, multiple regression and other multivariate analytic techniques have been employed to assess the independent effects of various factors on the probability and volume of pediatric utilization. The trend toward more rigorous analysis has been assisted by the increased sophistication of interview surveys at the local, state, and national levels.

THEORETICAL MODELS

Recent multivariate analyses have viewed health service utilization either as a process in and of itself, or as an input into the production of "health." Grossman (1972) developed a theoretical model of the demand for health, with health services representing one input into the health production function. Thus, the demand for health services is derived from the primary demand for health. Grossman and colleagues (1980) applied this model in an evaluation of the determinants of childrens' health. According to their economic model, parents act as utility maximizers in choosing between the quantity and quality of children, subject to wealth and price constraints as well

13

as their childrens' exogenous genetic endowments (which contribute to quality).

The following factors were expected to determine the level of childrens' health:

- the child's exogenous (genetic) health endowment,

- family wealth,

- parents' wage rates,

- family size,

- parents' educational attainment and other measures of their efficiency in household production,

- cost and availability of medical care and other market health inputs (vitamins, sanitation, etc.),

- the prices of inputs used to produce other aspects of child quality, and

- the prices of other forms of parents' consumption.

The model was empirically tested on a national sample of white children, ages 6 through 11, using data from the second National Health Examination Survey. Eleven health variables comprised the "output" measures, providing a multidimensional view of health.[2] The major finding pertained to the effect of income versus mother's schooling on childrens' health levels. The study found that the partial effect of income was generally not statistically significant, while mother's schooling consistently played an important role in determining health levels. Medical care use and availability were represented in the equations by dummy variables for the interval since last visit to a dentist. The use of preventive services (as measured by the dental visit proxies) was found generally to be associated with higher levels of health.

In contrast to Grossman's approach, most studies have focused on the derived demand for health services rather than the primary demand for health. The most widely cited framework for studying health services utilization was formulated by Andersen (1968) and refined by Andersen and Newman (1973) and Andersen, Kravitz, and Anderson (1975). This model aimed to integrate theories from the economic and sociological literatures on the translation of "need" into use.

The behavioral model is comprised of three groups of variables: predisposing, enabling, and need. (See Figure 1.) The predisposing component includes three subgroups of variables reflecting individual characteristics that are present prior to episodes of illness: demographic, social structural, and health beliefs. In the classical economic model, these variables reflect a consumer's "taste" for health services.

The enabling component includes both supply-side and demand-side factors that permit those predisposed to using services to actually do so. Family resources (e.g., income, insurance coverage, time costs, presence of a regular source of care) represent the traditional set of demand variables; community resource variables reflect time and money costs associated with use (e.g., physicians per population, region, residence).

The likelihood of using services is contingent not only upon the presence of predisposing and enabling conditions but also upon the perception of a need for services. Need is measured in this model through individual perceptions and clinical evaluations.

The relative importance of each of these variable groups tends to be related to the amount of discretion available to the individual (Andersen, 1968; Andersen and Newman, 1973). Need is the most important determinant where there is the least amount of discretion, for example, hospitalization. Where there is more discretion, as in the use of dental and other preventive services, predisposing and enabling factors are more important in determining who uses services and how much is used. Concerning overall physician utilization, need variables consistently have explained the greatest proportion of the variance, followed by demographic, social structure, and family resource characteristics. Variables reflecting health beliefs and community resources have been relatively unimportant in explaining physician use.[3]

A systematic review of the empirical findings on determinants of physician utilization follows, focusing on studies of the pediatric population, where possible. The discussion will be roughly organized around the "Andersen" framework:

- sociodemographic characteristics of the child and family--age, sex, race, family size, level of education, and marital status of the mother;

- economic factors--income, direct and indirect costs;

- organizational variables--existence and type of regular source of care, number of providers;

FIGURE 1

BEHAVIORAL MODEL OF HEALTH SERVICES USE
AND LIST OF VARIABLES WHICH OPERATIONALIZE THE COMPONENTS*

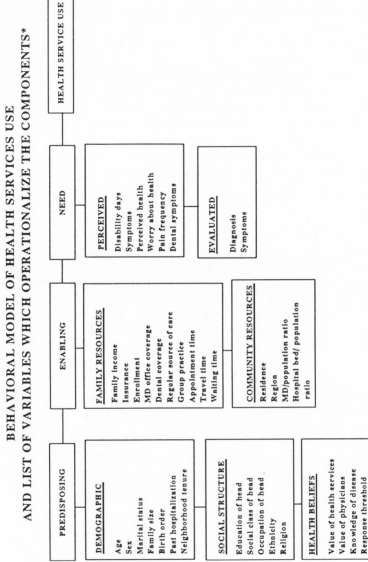

PREDISPOSING → ENABLING → NEED → HEALTH SERVICE USE

DEMOGRAPHIC

Age
Sex
Marital status
Family size
Birth order
Past hospitalization
Neighborhood tenure

SOCIAL STRUCTURE

Education of head
Social class of head
Occupation of head
Ethnicity
Religion

HEALTH BELIEFS

Value of health services
Value of physicians
Knowledge of disease
Response threshold

FAMILY RESOURCES

Family income
Insurance
Enrollment
MD office coverage
Dental coverage
Regular source of care
Group practice
Appointment time
Travel time
Waiting time

COMMUNITY RESOURCES

Residence
Region
MD/population ratio
Hospital bed/ population
  ratio

PERCEIVED

Disability days
Symptoms
Perceived health
Worry about health
Pain frequency
Dental symptoms

EVALUATED

Diagnosis
Symptoms

*This figure does not imply a causal relationship between use and the three major components
of the model (predisposing, enabling and need).
Adapted from: Andersen, Kravitz, and Anderson (1975), pp.5, 14-15.

• community resources--physician supply, physician participation in Medicaid, other community resources, residence, region;

• health status measurements; and

• other types of utilization--inpatient care, telephone call to physician.

Both descriptive and multivariate findings will be presented. Descriptive data provide unadjusted, baseline information on factors related to childrens' use of physicians. The data are from the 1980 National Health Interview Survey (NCHS, 1983a).[4] The multivariate studies permit a more rigorous analysis of the independent effects of specific variables, controlling for other variables specified in the model. The discussion includes studies that are limited to the pediatric population as well as selected studies covering the general population. Appendix 1 summarizes key features of the multivariate studies referenced in this chapter.

SOCIODEMOGRAPHIC CHARACTERISTICS OF THE CHILD AND FAMILY

Age

Age by itself does not predispose individuals to consume physicians' services. The relationship between age and utilization stems from such other factors as standards of medical practice (e.g., preventive services in infancy) and life cycle patterns (e.g., obstetrical or gynecological services in adolescence). Within the child population, there is a sharp age effect in the utilization of physicians' services. This effect takes the form of a U-shaped distribution, with use declining dramatically from birth through about age 10 or so and then rising during adolescence. However, visits to *pediatricians* do not demonstrate a U-shaped distribution, but rather continue to drop sharply with age (NCHS, 1983b).

This U-shaped age effect is not uniform for all population subgroups as demonstrated by data from the 1980 National Health Interview Survey (NCHS, 1983a). While utilization among males continues to decline into the twenties, physician visits among females increase during adolescence, the beginning of the childbearing years. A sharp increase is also seen for the lowest income subgroup (less than $5,000) at the onset of adolescence, compared to an ongoing decline for the highest income subgroup ($25,000 or more). Both blacks and whites appear to experience increases in use at approximately age 10.

A clear relationship also exists between age and use according to measures of health status. Those with no activity limitations and those in excellent or good health experience increases in physician visits at the onset of adolescence (again age 10 or so), while use continues to decline with age for those with some type of activity limitation or in fair or poor health.

Multivariate analyses of pediatric utilization consistently find an inverse relationship between age and utilization, holding other variables constant (Colle and Grossman, 1978; Goldman and Grossman, 1978; Inman, 1976; Tessler, 1980; Tessler and Mechanic, 1978; Wolfe, 1980). Wolfe posited a nonlinear relationship between use and age and included a quadratic age term (age-squared) in the regression equation. She found a positive and significant relationship between this variable and use, supporting the notion of a U-shaped age effect for childrens' use of health services.

Sex

As previously discussed, utilization by males and females is almost identical until adolescence. However, at about age 10 or so, males experience an ongoing decline in use while females begin to use more physicians' services, primarily for fertility-related needs. This pattern is also demonstrated by data from the National Ambulatory Medical Care Survey (NAMCS), a survey of visits to office-based physicians. In 1980-1981, the visit rate per 100 population for males was higher than for females from infancy through the early teens. Thereafter, females had a higher visit rate to pediatricians than males (NCHS, 1983b).

By and large, multivariate analyses of pediatric utilization have yielded nonsignificant coefficients on the sex variable. However, Colle and Grossman's (1978) study of a national sample of children ages 1 through 5 found that males had a significantly higher volume of private office-based physicians' services than females. Sex differences were not found in the probability of making any type of physician visit or more specifically, of seeking a preventive examination.

Another finding of sex differences in utilization was reported by Wolfe (1980). In an analysis of the percent of visits to specific types of providers, she found that males (ages 1 through 11) were more likely to use emergency rooms than females. There were no significant differences in the use of private practitioners, health centers, clinics, outpatient departments, and schools or other facilities.

Race

In 1980, black children of all ages made fewer physician visits than white children; among children under age 5, white children made an average of 7.5 visits versus 5.3 visits for black children. When income and health status are controlled for, the racial disparity intensifies (Kleinman et al., 1981).

Holahan's (1975) econometric analysis of racial differences in utilization among Medicaid eligibles indicated that nonwhites had fewer office-based physicians' visits than whites, when care was free and when controlling for income and education (among other factors). No significant race differences were found for physicians' services provided in outpatient hospital settings. Wolfe's (1980) study also found that nonwhites were significantly less likely to visit private physicians and more likely to visit health centers and clinics. However, no differences were found in the probability or volume of visits overall.

Early studies hypothesized that utilization differences resulted from negative attitudes towards health care among nonwhites or a lower value placed on health care. More recent studies point to organizational barriers or family structure as the mediating factors. The Congressional Budget Office (1977) reported that white/nonwhite utilization differences may result in part from financial barriers faced by nonwhites who are ineligible for Medicaid. In addition, four types of nonfinancial barriers were cited: (1) shortage of health resources in areas where nonwhites are concerned; (2) refusal by some providers to serve Medicaid recipients; (3) racial discrimination by providers; and (4) lack of knowledge or fear of discrimination on the part of potential users.

An alternate explanation is offered by Colle and Grossman (1978). They concluded that deficits among black children in the likelihood of a physician visit and/or a preventive examination are due, in large part, to lower levels of maternal education and larger family size.

Rossiter and Wilensky (1983) offer an interesting insight into racial differences in health service use. They divided visits according to whether the physician or the patient initiated contact. In a multivariate analysis that controlled for age, health status, income, and price, they found that, "blacks initiate fewer visits for themselves, but physicians also initiate fewer visits for blacks relative to whites."

Family Size

The theoretical relationship between the number of children in a family and the use of health services is complex. Becker and Lewis (1973) theorize that there is a negative correlation between the quantity and quality of children. They have formulated that the shadow price of children with respect to quantity (i.e., the cost of an additional child, holding quality constant) is greater, the higher their quality. Thus, the more children in the family, the more costly it may be to raise their average level of health. Given that per capita family income declines as family size increases, large families may use fewer services if demand is income elastic.

Another explanation of reduced demand among large families is that the household becomes more efficient in producing health. In other words, there may be a learning curve such that beyond a certain point, parents may be able to substitute for physicians in producing health. A third reason may be the greater inconvenience of seeking services with many young children in the household. As Lave and Leinhardt (1972) pointed out, "If a physician visit turns into an all-day affair both the nonmonetary and monetary costs of time lost are very high. A mother with small children must take all the children with her, or find and perhaps pay for a babysitter."

The empirical literature is quite consistent in noting an inverse relationship between number of children (or total household size) and utilization (Acton, 1975; Colle and Grossman, 1978; Davis and Reynolds, 1976; Goldman and Grossman, 1978; Kasper, 1975; Slesinger, 1976; Tessler, 1980; Wolfe, 1980).

Several studies provide additional insight into this relationship. Kasper (1975) found that utilization differences according to family size were exacerbated by other factors, as follows:

> Children in small families who are most likely to see a physician become even more likely to see a doctor when they are also high-income, other urban, one to five years old or white. Conversely, children least likely to see a physician--those who live in large families--become even less likely to see a doctor if they are also low-income, rural or inner city residents, older or nonwhite.

Davis and Reynolds (1976) found, in their comparison of those on welfare versus other low-income persons not on welfare, that family size was more of a constraint for welfare recipients. They speculated that this may be due to higher travel and waiting costs among those on welfare.

Tessler (1980) attempted to separate the effects of family size from the effects of birth order on utilization. He found that birth order had an independent effect and concluded, "The lower utilization observed among later-born children probably reflects their parents' increasing knowledgeability in regard to child care as well as their growing understanding of the uses and limitations of physicians' visits."

Level of Education

Two competing interpretations of the role of education have been advanced. The first suggests that education is a proxy for health beliefs and values (Rosenstock, 1966; Suchman, 1965). Higher levels of education are presumed to be associated with higher levels of utilization. The second views education, particularly maternal education as a proxy for household efficiency in the production of health (Grossman et al., 1980). As education increases, utilization will tend to decrease because the household is more efficient in producing health, perhaps through primary prevention of illness or accidents or through over-the-counter remedies. The first interpretation suggests a direct relationship between education and use, while the second view supports an inverse relationship.

The bivariate relationship between education and use is quite straightforward as education of the family head increases, the volume of visits increases. Children under age 5, for example, averaged 2.4 visits per year where the family head had less than 9 years of education, compared to 7.6 visits where the family head graduated high school and 8.6 visits where the family head graduated college (NCHS, 1983a).

Grossman and colleagues (1980) empirically tested the roles of the father's and the mother's schooling in relation to selected child health outcomes. They found that the effect of mother's schooling played a much more important role, signifying that this effect is behavioral rather than a proxy of genetic endowment. (Otherwise, equal effects would have been expected if parent's schooling represented genetic attributes.)

The relationship between mother's education and utilization is not uniform for all measures of use. Colle and Grossman (1978) found a positive relationship between mother's schooling and the likelihood of physician use as well as the likelihood of a preventive examination; in contrast, negative coefficients were obtained in the two volume equations. In other words, children of more highly educated mothers were more likely to visit a physician once but overall they made fewer visits. This finding is consistent with the second view of education as a proxy for household efficiency in producing health. In addition, the propensity of higher educated mothers to seek preventive services for their children suggests a possible substitution between preventive and curative services in these families.

Holahan (1975) focused specifically on the effect of education on utilization by Medicaid-eligible children. Using pooled 1969-1970 state-level data, he found that a higher education level (measured as the percent of the eligible population in a state who are high school graduates) was associated with lower rates of use of both office-based and hospital-based outpatient physicians' services. These findings support Holahan's hypothesis of a substitution effect between education and self-care or preventive care, as well as the reduction of unnecessary utilization. Holahan's results are consistent with those obtained by Colle and Grossman, although Holahan's study relies on state-level data and applies to children in a narrower income range.

Tessler (1980) also found that the mother's education was positively and significantly related to having a preventive exam, but was not associated with overall physician utilization. In contrast, Inman (1976) found that children whose mothers were college-educated had both more preventive and more curative visits than children whose mothers had a high school education or less.

Mother's Marital Status

Mother's marital status is a complex factor, representing both the tighter time constraints and the family stresses faced by single-parent families. Families with tighter time constraints may be less likely to use services due to the higher opportunity costs of time, all other things being equal; however, this may be counterbalanced by the tendency of daily stress to increase the probability of child health use (Roghmann and Haggerty, 1973; Tessler and Mechanic, 1978).

Few studies include mother's marital status as a determinant of pediatric utilization, and those that do tend to obtain insignificant coefficients (e.g., Inman, 1976). Wolfe found that children of "never married" mothers tended to have a higher volume of visits. However, she qualified these findings because of the small number of sample children with never married mothers. Children of "previously married" mothers were not significantly different from those in two-parent families. In general, mother's marital status does not appear to be an important factor associated with pediatric utilization.

ECONOMIC FACTORS

Income

Considerable amounts of research have been conducted to illucidate the income-use relationship. Descriptive analyses portray the relationship over time and across subpopulations. Multivariate studies test alternate hypotheses concerning the relationship between income and use (holding other variables constant). In addition, they provide estimates of the effect of income changes on the consumption of health care.

Data from the 1980 Health Interview Survey indicate that children in the lowest family income group (less than $5,000) had, on average, 4.4 physician contacts per year (including phone calls) compared to 4.0 contacts among those in the next income group ($5,000 to $9,999). Kovar (1982a) refers to this difference between poor and near poor children as the "so-called Medicaid effect." Children in higher income groups use slightly more services than the poorest children: 4.7 contacts ($10,000-$14,999); 4.5 contacts ($15,000-$24,999); and 4.5 contacts ($25,000 or more).

Kasper (1983) compared physician use by low-income children to that of higher-income children controlling for health status, insurance coverage, and type of regular source. Only low-income children under age 6 were as likely to have a physician visit as higher-income children. Low-income children ages 6 through 16 were less likely to see a physician. She attributes this to the impact of Medicaid on health service use by young children. Concerning preventive care, all low-income children under age 17 were at a disadvantage compared to higher-income children.

Kasper (1983) also compared the average number of visits for high income children to that for urban and rural low-income children. She found that low-income children under age 6 living in rural areas had one less visit than higher-income children. However, there were no differences between higher-income children ages 6 through 16 and rural low-income children ages 6 through 16. Furthermore, there were no differences in the number of visits for higher-income children and urban low-income children (under age 6 and ages 6 through 16).

Dutton (1978) used stepwise multiple regression to evaluate the association between income and pediatric utilization, controlling for five groups of variables: illness/demographic (stage I); family structure/socioeconomic factors (stage II); insurance coverage (stage III); health attitudes (stage IV); and type of usual source of care (stage V). She found that the association between income and use was independent of the socioeconomic and insurance variables (stages I, II, and III). After controlling for the attitude and health system variables (stages IV and V), Dutton concluded that income remained a strong determinant of the likelihood of any visit to the child's usual provider. In contrast, having positive health attitudes and using a private system of care eliminated the income differentials associated with the frequency of preventive care use.

Rundall and Wheeler (1979) used a similar analytic framework to test three alternate hypotheses concerning the effect of income on preventive care use by adults: (1) income-->use, testing the direct effect of financial constraints; (2) income-->health beliefs-->use, testing the indirect effect of attitudes (e.g., the "culture of poverty" hypothesis); and (3) income-->presence of a regular source of care-->use, testing the indirect effect of system barriers. The path analysis indicated that not having a regular source of care was the best explanatory variable in the income-use relationship.

Colle and Grossman (1978) and Wolfe (1980) found that income was an important determinant of some but not all types of utilization for some subpopulations. Colle and Grossman found a diminishing income effect with respect to the probability of physician utilization and the probability of a preventive checkup; family income was positively and significantly related to the number of private office visits. In another specification of the two probability equations, Colle and Grossman used two dummy income variables. They found that the middle and high-income groups were not significantly different from one another; however, the middle income group did have a significantly higher probability of both types of use than the low-income group.

Unlike Colle and Grossman, Wolfe found that family income was not a significant determinant of the probability or volume of physician use. However, in an analysis of the proportion of visits to each type of provider, income was a significant factor: children in families with incomes above 150 percent of poverty had a higher proportion of visits to private practitioners and outpatient departments and a lower proportion to health centers and clinics.

A family's responsiveness to changes in income (in terms of the quantity of a good consumed) is reflected in the "income elasticity," the percent change in consumption likely to result from a one percent change in income. Andersen and Benham (1970), using the family as the unit of analysis, found that the income elasticity in the simple income-use relationship was 0.41; when other variables were controlled for (price, quality, demographic characteristics, and use of preventive care), the income elasticity was reduced by nearly one-half to 0.22. Thus, as Dutton (1978) and Rundall and Wheeler (1979) have shown, other factors do mediate the income-use relationship, thereby reducing the estimates of income elasticity.

Studies that focus on pediatric utilization have obtained a wide range of income elasticity estimates. The differences in these estimates may be attributed to the scope of the samples, the specification of the models (particularly the operationalization of income), and the type of utilization being analyzed. By far the largest estimate was obtained by Goldman and Grossman (1978). They obtained an income elasticity of 1.318 for a private physician's office visit. (However, this study was based on a 1965-1966 sample of low-income children from New York City, prior to the implementation of Medicaid.)

Holahan (1975) derived income elasticities, based on a national sample of Medicaid eligible children and adults. The elasticities for children were much higher than for adults. He obtained an estimate of 0.56 for private office visits and 0.87 for hospital outpatient services. Colle and Grossman (1978) obtained an estimate of 0.38 for private office visits. Inman's (1976) estimates were the lowest: among the working mothers sample, the elasticity was in the 0.25 range; it was slightly lower, about 0.16, for the nonworking mothers sample.

Direct and Indirect Costs

MEASUREMENT ISSUES. The role of price in the use of pediatric care is difficult to measure. The existence of widespread third-party coverage for child health care (i.e., private insurance, Medicaid) has meant, at a minimum, that most parents are not sensitive to the price of care, and frequently are not even aware of the total amount charged to the payor(s). While out-of-pocket payments may be a proxy for the "money cost" to the uninsured and Medicaid recipients, it is an imperfect measure for the privately insured. In household interview surveys (upon which most of the relevant studies are based), out-of-pocket payments are retrospectively reported. However, the parent usually does not know upon entering the market, how much will be paid by the insurer and how much will ultimately be borne by the family. Where parents are required to pay the full fee "up front," out-of-pocket payments (as reported retrospectively) would not accurately reflect the price of care.

A proxy for "money cost" may be the presence of health insurance coverage. Frequently, however, this measure does not represent whether the family is reimbursed for office visits to physicians in private practice (and this should not be assumed). Further, the variation in copayment is omitted from such a simplistic operationalization.

Although Medicaid recipients have few, if any, out-of-pocket payments for medical care, they may face substantial nonmonetary costs. The privately insured and uninsured, too, face such indirect costs. For example, "time costs" are encountered in the form of travel time and waiting time in the doctor's office or clinic. Other indirect costs may be incurred in arranging and paying for transportation, obtaining information and searching for a provider, and scheduling an appointment (especially where substantial delays and inconvenience occur).[5] Each of these indirect costs represents potential non-price mechanisms for rationing care and may be important determinants of who initiates care, particularly as the importance of monetary outlays declines with the presence of third-party coverage (Acton, 1976).

"Money costs" most frequently have been approximated by a series of dummy variables for type of health insurance. The implicit assumption is that the privately insured face different costs than Medicaid recipients and the uninsured. Salkever (1976) refined this measure by accounting for the coinsurance rate for physicians' fees. Others (Anersen and Aday, 1978; Acton, 1976; Colle and Grossman, 1978) distinguished between those with coverage for private office visits and those lacking such coverage. Several studies included a measure of the average cost per physician visit based on either out-of-pocket costs (Inman, 1976) or total annual expenditures (Colle and Grossman, 1978; Goldman and Grossman, 1978; Wan and Soifer, 1974). A few of the studies omitted proxies for "money costs" altogether.

Marquis (1983) studied the accuracy of self-reporting on the extent of private insurance coverage for specific services. The analysis was based on 1,099 families with reported and verified insurance who were members of the experimental and control groups in the Rand Health Insurance Study. According to Marquis:

> . . . families were accurate in reporting their hospital care coverage but were less knowledgeable about their coverage for outpatient services. Lack of knowledge that outpatient services are covered is more likely among families whose policy includes a deductible than among families whose policies pay benefits for the first dollar expended.

Only 61 percent of the families with deductibles correctly reported that outpatient physician services were covered, compared to 87 percent with first dollar coverage and 92 percent with prepaid coverage. Marquis attributes this lower accuracy level, in part, to lack of knowledge as well as to a family's expectation that it will not satisfy the deductible and, hence, will not receive reimbursement. She noted, "Survey questions that probe about deductibles did result in fewer false negative responses among families whose policies include a deductible than did standard questions."

Similar findings have been reported for the National Medical Care Expenditure Survey. According to Berk et al. (1984), respondents were able to report accurately whether they had insurance, but were less familiar with the types of benefits covered by their policies. Specifically for ambulatory physician visits, 42 percent reported such coverage; a follow-up survey of employers and insurers revealed that 81 percent had such coverage.

Time costs were measured in three ways. The most sophisticated techniques entailed weighting travel and waiting times by the actual or imputed value of the person's time (in the case of pediatric studies, the mother's time). Another method involved entering separate variables for the travel/waiting times (usually measured in minutes) and the value of time (usually measured by dummy variables for occupational/educational status). A final approach used only one aspect of time costs--either the travel/waiting time or the value of time. Again, several studies omitted even the most rudimentary measure of time costs.

Other indirect costs--including those attributable to appointment delay, provider search, and transportation--received the most attention in the study by Colle and Grossman (1978). Other studies were most likely to include a measure for the availability of a regular source of care; however, many of these studies did not explicitly intend for this variable to reflect the time or other costs associated with seeing a provider. Tanner, Cockerham, and Spaeth (1983), for example, included type of regular source (public, private) to account for differences in care rendered in the two settings, not specifically the costs involved in entering the two systems.

EMPIRICAL FINDINGS. Feldstein's (1979) review of demand studies suggests that demand for physician services is price inelastic, with most of the estimates clustered between -0.1 and -0.2. However, the decision whether to use ambulatory care (especially preventive care) may be more price sensitive than decisions concerning the volume of visits (Davidson et al., 1980a).

The Rand Health Insurance Study provides the most recent evidence on the impact of income-related cost-sharing on expenditures for and use of child health services. Valdez et al. (1984) found that adjusted annual health care expenditures were one-third lower among children covered by cost-sharing plans ($260), compared to those in free plans ($345). In addition, children covered by cost-sharing plans had significantly lower use than those in free plans. The number of ambulatory visits varied by site, but overall children in free plans had one more visit than those in cost-sharing plans. The lower use and expenditures resulted primarily from differences in outpatient care; acute, chronic, and well care were all lower in cost-sharing plans.

Colle and Grossman (1978) found that the net price to the family[6] did not have a significant effect on the number of visits to a private, office-based physician, but it did negatively affect the average quality of visits (indexed by the mean office price of the type of physician seen, with general practitioners equal to one). Children receiving Medicaid benefits had office visits of lower average quality than those not on Medicaid, although Medicaid children had a significantly higher probability of overall physician use and preventive care use. The availability of private insurance for office visits was not significantly associated with the two probability equations.

Goldman and Grossman's (1978) analysis of office visits to private practice physicians investigated the nature of quantity-quality substitution in relation to changes in the quality-adjusted price and the fixed cost of a visit. The authors found that the "ratio of quality to visits falls as income and quality-adjusted price rise, and rises as the fixed cost of a visit rises. Moreover, visits are more responsive to a 1 percent change in fixed cost than to a 1 percent change in quality-adjusted price." The authors acknowledge that the income finding in counterintuitive.

Rossiter and Wilensky (1983) analyzed the factors associated with patient- and physician-initiated demand. The coinsurance rate, reflecting the amount paid by the family, had a negative effect on physician-initiated demand. This was interpreted as a reflection of the physician's role as agent. Patient-initiated demand, however, was not responsive to the magnitude of out-of-pocket payments.

Salkever's (1976) study of the demand for preventive care included a series of dummy variables of insurance coverage. The availability of insurance coverage for physician's fees did not consistently have a positive effect on demand. As expected, individuals paying between 1 and 50 percent out-of-pocket were more likely to have a physical examination than those paying over 50 percent. However, those with no copayments were less likely than the first group to have an exam, suggesting a possible substitution between curative and preventive services.

The time cost variables used by Colle and Grossman (1978) were not significantly related to pediatric utilization with one exception. The time cost for working mothers was negatively related to the likelihood of preventive care use. Increased transportation costs raised the "quality" and lowered the quantity of visits to physicians in private practice, as expected. Lack of a regular source decreased the probability of overall use, but did not significantly affect the use of preventive care, or the quantity or quality of private office visits. Lastly, appointment scheduling delay was not an important determinant of utilization.

Inman's (1976) study of physician utilization by children in Washington, D.C. concluded that the average travel and waiting time per doctor visit was one of the strongest determinants of the number of curative and preventive visits,[7] particularly for children whose mothers do not work. The average out-of-pocket fee did not significantly affect use for this subsample. Among the working mothers subsample, the average out-of-pocket expenditures alone or together with the cost of travel and waiting time (weighted by the imputed wage) were negatively associated with the volume of preventive and curative visits.

Wolfe (1980) tested the effect of time costs through two dummy variables reflecting the mother's employment status. She found that mothers who work full-time and mothers who are at home both take their children to physicians less frequently than other women (presumably those working part-time). The proxies for money cost--coverage under private insurance and Medicaid--were not significant determinants of volume of use.

Coffey (1983) studied the effect of time price on the demand for ambulatory female medical care. This analysis may have an application to the use of pediatric care since the mother frequently accompanies the child to the physician, and similar factors may influence a woman's demand for ambulatory female services and the demand for child health services. Based on a sample of 960 women ages 13 through 44 in Dallas County, Texas, Coffey derived a three equation demand model: likelihood of choosing a public provider, probability of entry for medical care, and volume of care. The time price (measured as an individual's market wage) negatively affected the decision to enter the medical care system, although the effect was minimal; the number of visits was not significantly affected by time price. Generally, health status measures were more important than the economic variables. Of particular note was the effect of time price on provider choice. The economic variables--time and money prices, distance, and eligibility for free care--were the primary determinants of the demand for a public source of care.

Three studies focusing on the general population provide additional insight into the role of time costs in the use of health services, although they are not directly generalizable to the pediatric population. Acton (1976) emphasized the role of time in the demand for health care by low-income New York City residents, due partly to the lack of data on money prices and also due to diminishing amounts of out-of-pocket payments. He found that travel and waiting times acted as normal prices. However, travel time had a greater effect on demand than waiting time, and overall, demand for public care was more sensitive to the length of travel and waiting times, than the demand for private care. Based on the time price elasticities derived in the analysis, Acton concluded that "time is already functioning as a rationing device for demand in this New York population, and its importance seems to exceed that of money prices."

In response to Acton's study, Luft, Hershey, and Morrell (1976) have suggested that the role of travel time may differ for urban and rural populations. In their study of Livingston County, California, travel time was a relatively unimportant factor in the use of health care. Where is was significant, it was positively related to use. The authors speculate, "although the distances may be greater, the travel times on uncrowded rural highways are often substantially shorter than in many urban areas. Also, the rural lifestyle may allow greater flexibility in scheduling and thus make travel time less of a barrier."

ORGANIZATIONAL VARIABLES

Existence and Type of Regular Source of Care

The existence of a regular source of health care lowers the marginal cost of a physician visit due to reduced time and information costs associated with finding a provider. In addition, those with a regular source may have greater physician input into the scheduling of periodic visits, such as well child exams. Thus, it is not surprising that numerous studies have shown that the presence of a regular source is associated with the use of physicians' services, especially preventive care (Andersen and Aday, 1976; Andersen, 1975; Salkever, 1976; Berki and Ashcraft, 1979; German et al., 1976; Tanner et al., 1983f, Kronenfeld, 1978b; Wan and Gray, 1978; Hershey et al., 1975). Moreover, this variable frequently has been considered the second most powerful determinant of physician utilization, following measures of health status.

The implications of these studies on the positive effect of a regular source of care should be qualified by two caveats. First, those who are high users of medical care may have a regular source precisely because of their high use. In such a case, the choice of a regular source may be a function of many of the same factors that are associated with utilization. Additionally, many surveys query respondents about the existence of a regular source of care at the point of interview, but then utilization data are collected for a prior time period. From a methodological standpoint, the coefficient on the regular source variable may be measuring the joint effect of other independent variables, while the coefficients on other variables may be biased towards zero.

Second, the choice of a regular source may reflect health beliefs that are not measured by other variables in the model; further, these beliefs may be associated with higher use, independent of having a regular source of care. The second caveat, therefore, is that those with a regular source may possess certain health beliefs that would predispose them to have a regular source and to use more health care. Both of these methodological caveats suggest that caution should be exercised in drawing policy implications concerning the effect of a regular source of care.

While the presence of a regular source of care tends to increase the probability of use, the effect is not uniform when type of regular source is disaggregated. Based on a sample of predominantly black children (under age 12) in Washington, D.C., Dutton (1979) derived use rates for five health care systems, adjusted for personal and family characteristics that would be expected to affect use. Comparisons of the adjusted use rates were made between the fee-for-service (FFS) solo practice and the four other systems of care. Dutton found that the frequency of preventive checkups was significantly higher among children enrolled in a prepaid group practice (PPGP), attending a public clinic, or using physicians in a group FFS practice, compared to children receiving care from physicians in a solo FFS practice. Checkups were lowest among children regularly using hospital outpatient departments or emergency rooms (OPD/ER). The probability of any type of care was highest among children enrolled in a PPGP and lowest in public clinics and hospital OPD/ERs. The use rates were not significantly different for children using a solo versus a group FFS practice.

In another study based on the same sample, Dutton (1978) sought to explain the relationship between income and use. She found that the type of regular source was a significant mediating factor in the income-use relationship. Specifically, enrollment in a PPGP had the strongest influence on use, while regular use of an OPD/ER had the strongest negative influence. Dutton concluded, "use rates are low among the poor in part because of inadequacies in the health care systems they use." Dutton's research points out the importance of specifying the type of regular source, not merely whether or not the child had a regular source.

Kasper (1983) also focused on the effect of the type of regular source on childrens' access to physicians. However, instead of analyzing the type of setting, Kasper distinguished between having and not having a regular physician.[8] For young children (under age 6), those with a regular place who did not see a specific doctor had lower rates of use than those having a private physician as a regular source. In contrast, children ages 6 through 16 with a regular place (regardless of whether they saw a specific physician) were not significantly different from those with a private physician. As expected, low-income children with no regular source were least likely to have any physician visit or a preventive visit. This study suggests that for low-income children under age 6 the presence of a regular physician (either office-based or clinic-based) is important, while for children ages 6 through 16 simply having a usual source of care (not necessarily a specific physician) increases utilization.

Skinner et al. (1978) examined utilization patterns among adults in a low-income community in East Baltimore, Maryland. They noted the importance of enrollment in a health maintenance organization in reducing utilization differentials between Medicaid recipients and the near poor not on Medicaid. Compared to users of a hospital outpatient department and other sources, HMO enrollees had the highest probability of ambulatory care use and the highest volume of visits.

Marcus and Stone (1984) also studied the effect of type of regular source. Using data from the Los Angeles Health Survey, they examined differences in rates of physician visits among adults who were enrolled in a health maintenance organizations compared to those using fee-for-service providers. Initial analyses revealed no significant differences among the FFS and HMO groups in the "proportion of total reported health problems resulting in a doctor contact." However, when differences in having a regular doctor were controlled, HMO enrollees had a significantly higher utilization rate. The authors suggest that having a regular doctor (not just a regular source) promotes patient-provider continuity which in turn stimulates medical care use.

Number of Providers

A study by Hennelly and Boxerman (1979) adds another dimension to the relationship between a regular source and physician utilization. They hypothesized that a lack of continuity (e.g., use of multiple providers) would lead to inefficient utilization. To test this hypothesis, they used a national sample of individuals who reported a physicians as a regular source of care and who had an illness episode not requiring hospitalization, but involving at least two physician visits. Through an analysis of variance model, they found that the number of visits increased as continuity was reduced. Those who used multiple sources of care had more visits than those with a single source. Clinic users made more visits than those using solo or group practice physicians. While generalization of these findings is limited due to the large number of chronic cases in the sample, the study suggests that a regular source of care may decrease the volume of use among some populations.

Kronenfeld (1980) also demonstrated that complex "provider set patterns" are associated with higher use, perhaps due to a lack of continuity of care. For example, of the respondents reporting a family or general practitioner as the primary affiliation, those with multiple affiliations had an average of 3.3 visits compared to 1.8 visits among these with only a primary affiliation. These averages were adjusted for number of conditions, disability days, payment source, income, education, sex, and age.

Neither of the above-mentioned studies evaluates the "appropriateness" of visits to multiple providers. Fletcher et al. (1984) noted that, in some cases, seeing multiple providers can result in duplication and overlap, but in others, a team approach can achieve better results. Thus, they devised a classification scheme reflecting the integration of care. Care was considered integrated if (1) the visit was made to the primary physician (i.e., continuous care); or (2) if there was written evidence that the primary physician knew about the visit and the nonprimary physician was aware of the primary physician's involvement. Fletcher et al. suggest that future studies should include a measure of coordination or integration of care, not merely continuity of care.

COMMUNITY RESOURCES

Physician Supply

Physician-population ratios are frequently used as a measure of physician availability. This measure has been criticized because it masks geographic and population heterogeneity across counties; ignores physician specialty mix and practice patterns; and overlooks the contributions of nonphysician personnel.

Generally, studies that have shown a positive and significant relationship between physician supply and demand for health care have used supply data aggregated to the state level and have obtained state-level proxies for individual demand characteristics (Fuchs and Kramer, 1972; Holahan, 1975). However, when the demand characteristics are observed directly for individuals and supply characteristics are measured at the county or state level, it is more difficult to detect underlying relationships on the supply variables. For this reason, many multivariate studies have found demand characteristics (e.g., health status, age) to be far more important than supply factors in determining utilization (Andersen et al., 1983; Andersen and Newman, 1973).

Chiu, Aday, and Andersen (1981) studied the discriminatory power of physician-population ratios in predicting health service use between physician shortage and nonshortage areas. As expected, those in shortage areas had longer travel and waiting times and lower probabilities of having any physician contact or of regular sources of care. The volume of visits and the likelihood of obtaining preventive care were not significantly different.

Berk, Bernsetin, and Taylor (1983) replicated the study by Chiu et al. with a more precise designation of shortage areas (according to ZIPcodes rather than counties) and using multivariate analytic techniques. Compared to the earlier study, Berk et al. concluded "these inequities are better explained by differences in income, racial composition, and insurance coverage between shortage and nonshortage populations than by differences in physician manpower."

Holahan's (1975) state-level study of Medicaid-eligibles found that the availability of office-based physicians was not a significant factor in pediatric utilization. In contrast, the availability of hospital-based physicians was significantly related to outpatient hospital use. Holahan suggests that areas with high ratios of office-based physicians per population may also have more outpatient resources, thus wiping out the effect of office-based physician availability. The significant effect of outpatient resources may be due to lower time costs or a higher perceived quality of care.

Colle and Grossman (1978) found that physician stock was positively related to the probabilities of overall use and of a preventive examination, as well as to the quality of visits. The volume of visits was not significantly affected by physician availability. They note that these findings are not consistent with a model of supplier-induced demand, since the volume of visits appears to be unaffected by physician supply.

Wolfe (1980) used median census tract income as a proxy for provider availability. This measure was positively related to the probability of any physician visit, and particularly to a physician in office-based practice. It was negatively associated with the percent of visits to health centers and clinics. These results reflect the tendency for such facilities to locate in lower-income tracts and for private physicians not to practice in these areas.

Three studies suggest that Medicaid recipients face a different market for physicians' services than the privately insured population. In the first study, Colle and Grossman (1978) used a dummy variable for Medicaid which yielded a negative coefficient in the equation for quality of visits. As discussed previously, the authors interpreted this as an indication of barriers to care provided by physicians in private practice, particularly specialists. They concluded, "the sizable quality differential can be attributed to the failure of many Medicaid reimbursement schedules to recognize physician specialty."

In the second study, Davis and Reynolds (1976) obtained different results on the supply variable for the public assistance and other low-income subpopulations. Physician supply had a positive effect on use by the other low-income persons; it was not significantly related to use by those receiving public assistance. Davis and Reynolds attribute this nonsignificant finding, in part, to the inappropriateness of an aggregate measure of physician supply "since the poor may be restricted to a subset of all providers such as county hospitals or those physicians practicing in low-income neighborhoods."

Finally, Holahan (1975) found that the mechanism for physician reimbursement under Medicaid was an important factor in the use of office-based physician services (but not outpatient hospital use). In states using fee schedules (versus usual, customary, and reasonable charges) as a basis for Medicaid reimbursement of office-based physicians, Medicaid-eligible children had lower rates of use. The implication of this finding is that office-based physicians tend to be sensitive to the reimbursement rate under Medicaid in deciding whether to accept Medicaid patients, and if so, how many. The next section explores the determinants of physician participation in Medicaid.

Physician Participation in Medicaid

Unpublished data from the LaJolla Medicaid Program Characteristics Data File indicate that the rate of physician participation in Medicaid varied widely among the states in 1981, ranging from 6.19 physicians per 1,000 Medicaid recipients in South Carolina and 7.82 in Maine, up to 36.86 physicians per 1,000 residents in Montana and 157.08 in Nebraska.[9] Specifically among pediatricians, a 13-state study conducted by the American Academy of Pediatrics found wide variation in the percent of pediatricians reporting acceptance of Medicaid patients, with a low of 52 percent in Georgia to a high of 100 percent in Iowa, and a median of 95 percent (Davidson, et al., 1980b). The average level of Medicaid participation in the 13 states (measured as the percent of a physician's practice paid for by Medicaid), ranged from 7 percent (Tennessee) to 32 percent (California), with a median of 13 percent.

Several multivariate analyses have been conducted recently to examine the physician characteristics and state program policies associated with Medicaid participation among physicians. Sloan, Mitchell and Cromwell (1978) concluded that the decision to participate in Medicaid "reflects a mix of demand, supply, and Medicaid policy factors." Based on a sample of general practitioners, pediatricians, internists, general surgeons, and obstetricians/gynecologists, the authors found that physician involvement was sensitive to the relative fee schedules under Blue Cross and Medicaid, and by inference, Medicare. Medicaid participation was also found to be a function of collection costs (e.g., delay in payments, time spent filling out claim forms); size of the Medicaid-eligible pool in the community; the wage of nonphysician personnel; physician credentials (i.e., foreign medical graduate); and physician attitudes toward "health care as a right." General practitioners and pediatricians had higher participation rates than internists, general surgeons, and obstetricians.

Mitchell (1983) examined the determinants of Medicaid participation by medical and surgical specialists. Like the primary care physicians studied by Sloan, Mitchell and Cromwell (1978), specialists were sensitive to the reimbursement levels under Medicaid and Blue Shield. In addition, the probability or level of participation among specialists was highest in states that contracted with fiscal agents for claims processing; that imposed no requirements for prior authorization or no quantity limits on the supply of specific services; and that extended Medicaid coverage to the medically indigent. Physicians practicing in counties with low per capita incomes or high physician-population ratios were less likely to treat Medicaid patients. Physician characteristics associated with Medicaid participation included type of specialty (i.e., surgical specialists generally had higher rates of participation than medical specialists) and physician age, with younger and older physicians participating at a higher rate than "middle age" physicians.

The importance of economic incentives on physician participation in Medicaid was underscored by Hadley (1979). Using data from the California Medicaid program, he analyzed the percentage of physicians participating in Medicaid and the average Medicaid caseload among participating physicians. The county was the unit of analysis. Hadley concluded, "the most significant finding is the reaffirmation of the importance of the amounts of both private charges and Medicaid payments in determining participation rates and average Medicaid caseloads per participating physician."

In another study, Mitchell and Schurman (1982) investigated the factors associated with Medicaid participation among pediatricians. The ratio of office-based physicians per 1,000 population had an unexpected negative effect on the decision to participate. Also unexpectedly, pediatricians were not sensitive to the level of Medicaid fees. Being board-certified, a Third World foreign medical graduate, female, and young were all significantly associated with Medicaid participation. The size of the Medicaid eligible pool in the county was another positive influence.

Davidson, et al. (1983) found that the average statewide fee for a well-child office visit was positively and significantly related to the extent of a pediatrician's participation in Medicaid. Other variables that were found to differentiate full participants from limited participants[10] included the level of nonphysician personnel costs, practicing in a metropolitan area, and number of weeks between billing and payment, all of which were inversely related to full participation in Medicaid. In addition, full participants were likely to practice in states with higher scores on the Revised Medicaid Program Index, a proxy for professional incentives under Medicaid.[11]

Given the evidence on the relationship between Medicaid reimbursement levels and physician participation in Medicaid,[12] it is instructive to review available data on reimbursement rates for pediatricians. The Urban Institute gathered data from each state on average payments for 61 procedures. Fee indices were calculated by weighting procedures according to their relative importance and then aggregating across procedures. For the pediatrics fee index, six procedures were included: brief exam, limited exam, and intermediate exam for established patients; brief hospital visit; limited hospital visit; and routine newborn care in hospital. The average fee for pediatrics was $15.62, with a range among states of $5.76 to $33.61 (Holahan, 1982b).

In another analysis, Holahan (1984) compared state Medicaid fees to Medicare prevailing charges. Ten states paid general practitioners the same rate under Medicaid and Medicare. In 20 states, the Medicaid fee was less than 80 percent of the Medicare prevailing charge. Five states paid more under Medicaid relative to the Medicare usual, customary, and reasonable charge.

Other Community Resources

None of the multivariate studies listed in Appendix 1 included measures of other health resources, such as outpatient departments or emergency rooms. In particular, the availability of such facilities would be expected to significantly affect use by uninsured low-income children as well as use by Medicaid children in communities with low physician participation in Medicaid.

A study by Kovar (1982), using data from the 1975 and 1976 National Health Interview Surveys found that the presence of an outpatient department in the county of residence was associated with a child's probability of receiving adequate medical care. The presence of an emergency room was not a significant factor.

On a more descriptive level, a General Accounting Office (1975) study found that physician scarcity in two inner city, low-income neighborhoods was responsible for the high use of outpatient hospital care and publicly-financed health centers.

Place of Residence

Residence in a Standard Metropolitan Statistical Area (SMSA) has been used as a proxy for differences in the availability of providers, and hence ease of entry into the medical care system. Data from the 1980 National Health Interview Survey indicate that the highest utilization occurred among children residing within SMSAs, but outside the central city. Kleinman (1981) found especially dramatic differences in the volume of visits between metropolitan and nonmetropolitan residents when race and health status were considered. Using data from the 1976-1978 National Health Interview Surveys, he found that children under age 17 in fair or poor health who lived in metropolitan areas had an average of 11.6 contacts compared to 8.4 contacts among those in rural areas. Differences between whites and blacks were even more striking. In metropolitan areas white children had 13.4 contacts versus 8.1 contacts by black children; in rural areas the comparable figures were 10.1 contacts versus 3.5 contacts.

Since most of the multivariate analyses on pediatric utilization used samples that were local in scope, "place of residence" has not frequently been tested as a determinant of utilization. The studies by Holahan (1975) and Colle and Grossman (1978) are the exceptions. Holahan found that SMSA residence was not a significant factor in office-based physician use among Medicaid-eligible children. However, children living in SMSAs had higher rates of use of outpatient hospital services. Holahan explains the meaning of these results as follows:

> These differences in the utilization of ambulatory services do not appear to result from substitution of hospital outpatient care for medical services, for the SMSA variable indicates no difference in the latter for SMSA and non-SMSA residents. Since there is no greater use of outpatient services and difference in use of medical services, it appears that SMSA residents receive more ambulatory care than Medicaid eligibles living in rural areas. Thus distance and accessibility do affect utilization, unless location of residence is associated with differences in either attitudes toward medical care, or the need for medical services.

Colle and Grossman consider place of residence an intermediate variable for testing interactions between physician availability (ratio of physicians per 1,000 population) and residence. They found a significant interaction for the two equations on probability of ambulatory use and of a preventive examination, but not for the volume of visits. The coefficients for the MD-interaction variables were uniformly larger in the ten largest SMSAs than in other SMSAs and other urban (non-SMSA) areas.

Multivariate studies in the general population suggest that place of residence may not be an important determinant of utilization once other variables are controlled for. Wan and Soifer (1974) constructed a path analysis, based on data from a 1972 household survey of five counties in New York and Pennsylvania. Residence in an urban area had an insignificant effect on volume of visits. Wolinsky's (1978) path analysis using National Health Interview Survey data from 1971, 1972, and 1973 also yielded insignificant results on the residence variables.

Two studies provide possible explanations for the nonsignificance of "place of residence" variables. First, Williams, et al. (1983) suggest that distances of rural populations (towns of less than 25,000 population) from medical and surgical specialists have declined substantially. For example, the rural population living within 20 "straight-line" miles (about 25 minutes) from a pediatrician increased from 62 percent in 1970 to 71 percent in 1979. They estimated that 98 percent of the rural population was within 20 miles of a general/family practitioner in both 1970 and 1979. There is also evidence that rural populations may be willing to travel further to a doctor, if necessary, as Luft, Hershey, and Morrell (1976) discovered in their study of Livingston County, California. Based on these studies, rural residence, by itself, does not appear to impede access.

Geographic Region

In national studies of physician utilization, geographic region has been proposed as another proxy for availability of resources. Davis and Rowland (1983) suggest that geographic region may also be associated with insurance status. In the South and West, the percent uninsured during the year is twice that of the Northeast and North Central regions. They attribute these differences to the effects of unionization in northern industrial states.

Data from the 1980 National Health Interview Survey show that volume of use does indeed vary across regions. Children under age 5 living in the West have the lowest volume of use; among children ages 5 through 14, those who live in the South have the lowest use (NCHS, 1983a).

Davis and Reynolds (1976) found that geographic region (i.e., residence in the South) was important in explaining utilization differences among blacks. Blacks on welfare who lived in the South had higher predicted levels of utilization than black welfare recipients outside the South. However, Southern blacks not on welfare had lower predicted levels of utilization than non-welfare blacks outside the South. These results should be interpreted with caution since the study was based on data from 1969.

Using data from 1977, Davis and Rowland (1983) present more recent evidence on physician visits among those under age 65, according to race, residence, and insurance status. Blacks outside the South continued to have a slightly higher number of physician visits per year than Southern blacks (3.5 versus 2.8 among those who were insured). The largest difference, however, is between insured blacks living outside the South (3.5 visits) and uninsured Southern blacks (1.5 visits), a ratio of 2.33. Whites had lower regional differences, controlling for insurance status.

HEALTH STATUS

Measurement Issues

The concept of health status has been operationalized in numerous ways. Most studies use more than one measure, including perceived health status, chronic conditions, self-reported symptoms, hospitalization, and days of disability or restricted activity. Several of these measures, especially perceived health status, disability days, and restricted activity days, frequently have been criticized as imperfect proxies for "need" for health services.

First, measurement bias or error may result when health status measures contain a psychosocial or psychocultural component that is unintended. Because health status measures are self-reported, they are highly dependent on an individual's health beliefs or cultural background. For example, the relationship between assessment of symptoms and cultural background has been proposed by Zola (1964), Rosenblatt and Suchman (1966), and others. McKinlay and Dutton (1974) suggested that what is considered a measure of "need" in utilization studies, perceived health status, is highly dependent on an individual's definition of illness and the value placed on health. Similarly, Mechanic (1979) noted that "what are characterized as 'illness' variables in the multivariate studies are more appropriately seen as illness-behavior measures incorporating various learned inclinations, value orientations, and life events as well as physical illness." Regarding the health status of children, the perception and values of the respondent (usually the mother) contribute to the reporting of child health status.

A second measurement issue concerns the multidimensionality of health status. Because health status is a latent concept, several researchers have cautioned against the use of a single measure.

Brunswick (1975) used principal components analysis to develop a measure of adolescent health status, based on survey data from 671 black Harlem residents, ages 12 through 17. The data analysis produced four factors: (1) morbidity--number of self-reported health problems; (2) attitude--self-rating of health; (3) functional limitation--with respect to activities in and out of school; and (4) disability--number of school-loss days. Brunswick concluded that such a multiple-item indicator of adolescent health status was more reliable and conceptually meaningful than a single-item indicator.

Eisen, et al. (1979) described a "state of the art" questionnaire developed for the Rand Health Insurance Study to measure child health status. Questions dealt with five aspects of health: physical health (i.e., functional limitations), mental health, social relations, general health perceptions, and parent's satisfaction with child's development. The authors found a very small number of children had either chronic or acute limitations of activity so they were unable to construct a physical health scale. However, the remaining scales possessed sufficient variability to discriminate between those with limitations and those with none. They concluded that the multiple-item scales were more reliable and valid than single-item indicators.

In another analysis based on data from the Rand Health Insurance Study, Manning et al. (1982) evaluated the gains in explanatory power from a comprehensive model as opposed to the traditional "excellent/good/fair/poor" (EGFP) measure of perceived health status. The proportion of explained variance for adults' outpatient expenditures increased from 12.9 percent to 18.4 percent when the single EGFP measure was replaced by the full model.

A final problem with most measures of health status is that they are collected concurrently with measures of health service use. This is a problem particularly with measures of disability or restricted activity days and self-reported symptoms. For example, a problem of simultaneity may arise when restricted activity leads to a physician visit that then results in continued activity restriction. The direction of causality is ambiguous between disability and utilization.

This phenomenon is illustrated by Wilson and White (1977), based on cross-sectional time-series data. From 1964 to 1973, the number of physician visits per child in the United States increased substantially among poor children, approaching or exceeding the rate for the nonpoor. During this same time period, the average number of school-loss days among poor children also rose. The authors point out that this does not necessarily reflect higher illness levels among the poor; the reported increase in activity restriction may have resulted from greater access to physicians. As Wilson (1981) comments:

> . . . increased access to health care can result in physician-ordered activity restriction (bed-days, school-loss days, work-loss days), whereas without the care there might have been less activity restriction but more discomfort or risk of permanent damage to the health of the individuals.

Manning et al. (1982) estimated the effect of using current health measures to "postdict" utilization in a previous time period. This analysis was based on preliminary data from the Rand Health Insurance Study. They found that postdicting empirically moves the coefficients away from zero; in all but two cases they were larger in absolute value. Additionally, postdicting raises the amount of explained variance. In light of these findings, they offer the following practical advice:

> Many researchers will not be able to avoid the problem of analyzing health status variables from a period subsequent to their measures of utilization. If possible, one would like to

> treat such health status variables as endogenous. But it is difficult to think of good instrumental variables . . . . At a minimum, one should be aware of the problem. Furthermore, one should use all the health status variables at hand, but the natural tendency would be to do this anyway . . .

Nevertheless, Goldstein, Siegel, and Boyer (1984) offer some encouragement concerning the use of a single-item index of perceived health status. Using data from the 1976-1977 Los Angeles Health Survey, they examined factors associated with changes in perceived health status. They concluded that the index was not significantly associated with indicators of: (1) objective health status, (2) health beliefs, (3) health practices, or (4) utilization of health services. The authors suggest, "the underlying social psychological perception (the index) reflects is a sensitivity to chronic illness of long standing. It is not sensitive to short-term changes in objective health status, be they acute illness or the beginning of chronic illness, even when these illnesses necessitate contact with providers or limitation of normal activities."

Empirical Findings

Available data suggest that "greater severity of illness as well as higher prevalence of certain conditions is present among poor children" (Egbonu and Starfield, 1982). Compared to nonpoor children, poor children have higher rates of hospitalization; are at higher risk of death; have more severe acute illnesses (as indicated by restricted activity days, school-loss days, and bed-days); and have higher rates of prematurity and its sequelae.

As health status declines, health service use is expected to increase. In fact, 1980 National Health Interview Survey data support this notion (NCHS, 1983a). Among children under age 5 with no activity limitation, the average number of physician contacts was 6.8; those with any type of activity limitation averaged 22.0 contacts. The same magnitude of difference was found for children ages 5 through 14 with limitations versus those without. The inverse relationship between health status and use was also found with respect to number of bed-days in the previous year and perceived health status. On average, children under age 5 in excellent, good, fair, or poor health had 6.0, 7.6, 18.5 and 30.3 physician contacts, respectively. (It should be noted that the health status measures correspond to a period following the physician contacts, and can therefore be an "effect" rather than a "cause" of such contact.)

Variables representing individual health status have consistently yielded the highest explanatory power in multivariate analyses of utilization within the general population (Acton, 1976; Andersen, 1975; Hershey et al.,

1975; Kronenfeld, 1980; Wan and Soifer, 1974; and Wolinsky, 1978). This has been found internationally, as well (Bice and White, 1969).

Among children, indicators of health status are significant determinants of utilization but not necessarily the most important factors (e.g., Colle and Grossman, 1978; Inman, 1976; Wolfe, 1980). This is most likely due to the discretionary component of preventive and acute care, as well as the insensitivity of most child health status measures to the "need" for well-child care. In fact, Colle and Grossman (1978) found that children in excellent health were more likely to use preventive services than children in good, fair, or poor health. Salkever (1976), Lairson and Swint (1978) and Runally and Wheeler (1979) also found a positive relationship between preventive care use and health status in their studies of the general population.[13]

Smythe-Staruch et al. (1984) compared the health service use of chronically ill and disabled children (n = 369) and a comparison group of non-disabled children (n = 456) in Cleveland, Ohio. The mean number of health and related visits was ten times higher among children with chronic conditions (78.8 visits) compared to the control group (7.8 visits). More specifically:

- Chronically ill children were slightly more likely to see a physician in the previous year (98 percent) relative to the comparison group (88 percent). Moreover, children with chronic conditions were twice as likely to see physician specialists (79 percent versus 42 percent).

- The volume of physician visits was much higher among chronically ill children, averaging 8.9 visits in the previous year, compared to 3.3 visits among the control group.

- The percentage with at least one dental visit was also significantly higher among chronically ill children (69 percent) than the control group (61 percent).

- Chronically ill children had substantially higher use of occupational, physical, and speech therapist services, as well as mental health and social services (particularly social workers).

- The two groups did not differ significantly in the proportion having contact with a school nurse;

however, among users, chronically ill children averaged 29.4 visits versus 2.1 visits for the control group.

- Hospitalization rates were much higher for the chronically ill and disabled children (34 percent) versus the comparison group (6 percent).

OTHER UTILIZATION

Inpatient Care

In this era of high medical care costs, proposals abound for shifting the locus of health services from inpatient care, to less costly ambulatory care. The central issue revolves around whether outpatient care represents a substitute or complement for inpatient care. According to Frieberg (1979), "the weight of the research to date suggests that the complementary effect of outpatient services appears to outweigh the substitution effect." The studies that support a "substitution effect" tend to be based on aggregated data, such as states (Davis and Russell, 1972); health service areas in one state (Brewer and Freedman, 1982) or most states (Gold, 1984); or physicians (Rosenblatt and Moscovice, 1984). Studies that use the individual as the unit of observation generally do not find a substitution effect between inpatient and outpatient care; rather a complementarity appears to exist, such that the two types of utilization are positively related.

In a now classic study of the demand for hospital outpatient care, Davis and Russell (1972) found that such demand was sensitive to the inpatient occupancy rate, and furthermore, that the cross-price elasticities between inpatient and outpatient care were significant and negative. According to their estimates, reducing the price of outpatient care by 10 percent would reduce the admission rate by 1.6 percent and raise the outpatient visit rate by 7.5 percent. Gold (1984) replicated the Davis and Russell analysis using more recent data (1978 versus 1969) that were disaggregated to the health service area level (as opposed to the state level). She confirmed the Davis and Russell findings of a negative cross-price elasticity for inpatient and outpatient care.

A substitution effect was also found in a study be Brewer and Freedman (1982). Health service areas in Vermont with high levels of outpatient care use had significantly lower hospitalization rates. Further analysis indicated this relationship was due to sociodemographic characteristics of the area rather than the population's health status and hospital bed supply.

A recent study by Rosenblatt and Moscovice (1984) also supported the inverse relationship between hospitalization and hospital occupancy rates.

In addition, physicians with busier outpatient practices have lower hospitalization rates: physicians in lower per capita income counties have higher rates of hospitalization.

Among preschool children, Colle and Grossman (1978) found that hospitalization had a significant and positive relationship to the probability of any physician use and the number of quality-adjusted visits. No relationship was found between inpatient care use and preventive use or the overall volume of visits. The study by Goldman and Grossman (1978) found that hospitalization was directly related to both the overall number of visits and the number of quality-adjusted visits. Similarly, Wolfe (1980) found that hospitalization was significantly and positively related to the probability and volume of use. However, inpatient care use was not significantly related to the type of ambulatory care provider used.

Berki and Ashcraft (1979) explain the direct relationship between hospital days and illness visits by noting, "episodes of illness requiring hospitalization on a nonemergency basis usually include preadmission and post-discharge ambulatory phases."

Unlike other studies, Acton (1976) obtained conflicting results in his analysis of two low-income neighborhoods in New York City. He reported, "in Red Hook . . . inpatient and outpatient care seem to be operating as substitutes. The longer one must wait for ambulatory care, the more likely one is to use inpatient care. The opposite appears to be true in Bedford-Crown. It is not clear why this difference exists at this level of analysis, but it may be compatible with the hypothesis that residents of Bedford-Crown are seeking care only for the more serious health conditions, and in those cases, inpatient and outpatient care are complements."

Telephone Call to Physicians

Over one-fifth (21.4 percent) of all physician contacts by children under age 5 were telephone consultations; among children ages 5 through 14 telephone consultations represented 14.8 percent of all physician contacts (NCHS, 1983a). The relationship between a telephone consultation and a face-to-face contact has rarely been explored in studies of pediatric utilization.

Kovar (1982b) found that having a telephone was an important distinguishing feature between children with at least one physician contact in the previous year, and those with none. For example, 87 percent of the children in homes with phones had adequate medical care (determined according to interval of last visit) compared to 76 percent of those without telephones. The difference is even greater when the family size and interval since the mother's last visit are considered. It is not clear whether having a telephone is a proxy for certain socioeconomic characteristics of the family or whether it actually measures the likelihood of a telephone call to a physician.

Pope et al. (1971) studied physician utilization in a prepaid group plan in Portland, Oregon and found that a large proportion of medical care was provided over the phone. They noted that this was not solely related to the availability of a phone. They conclude, "Studies that treat contacts with physicians in an undifferentiated way or attempt to explain physician utilization without considering the mode of contact will fail to discern the actual impact of various social or demographic factors on utilization."

NOTES

1. Among the early studies were: Alpert, Robertson, Kosa, et al., 1976; Bullough, 1974; Gold and Rosenberg, 1974; Haggerty, Roghmann, and Pless, 1975; Hochheiser, Woodward, and Charney, 1971; Kelman and Lane, 1976; Leopold, 1974; Levey, Bonnano, Schwartz and Sanofsky, 1979; Okada and Wan, 1980; Roghmann, 1975; Salber, Feldman, Rosenberg, and Williams, 1971; and Scherzer, Druckman, and Alpert, 1980.

2. The eleven child health measures were: parental assessment of children's health, height, weight, hearing acuity, visual acuity, blood pressure, hayfever or allergies, parental assessment of tension, presence of one or more significant acquired abnormalities on physical exam, periodontal index, and excessive school absence for health reasons in last six months.

3. These studies employed a technique known as "multiple classification analysis." This technique evaluates the relative importance of the variable groups, measuring the additive and cumulative effects of the independent variables on the dependent variables. The method does not take into account interaction effects.

4. Although more recent Health Interview Survey data are available, 1980 was chosen since it corresponds to the time period of the data set used in this study.

5. A fourth type of cost was identified by Lave and Leinhardt (1972): "the psychological costs generated by the encounter with providers." These costs are not directly quantified in multivariate studies.

6. The net price to the family was calculated by dividing the total annual expenditures by the total number of visits and then multiplying that figure by the coinsurance rate for physicians' fees.

7. Inman's findings differ from the results obtained by Colle and Grossman concerning the effect of time costs on nonworking mothers. This may be a local phenomenon that "washes out" in a national study.

8. Kasper (1983) compares four types of arrangements: physician's office as a regular office; another place with a regular doctor; another place without a regular doctor; and no regular source of care.

9. The data for Maine are for 1980; the data for Nebraska include out-of-state physicians participating in the state's Medicaid program.

10. Davidson, et al. (1983) define full participation as those who reported accepting all new non-Medicaid and Medicaid patients. Limited participants accept all new non-Medicaid patients and some new Medicaid patients. This analysis excluded all physicians reporting that they did not accept any Medicaid patients as well as those reporting that they did not accept all new non-Medicaid patients.

11. The Revised Medicaid Program Index summarizes aspects of professional incentives that were expected to have a positive relationship with the extent of Medicaid participation. According to Davidson, et al. (1983):

> When Medicaid policies impinge upon professional autonomy, interfering with the exercise of professional judgment and the ongoing physician-patient relationship, the physician is expected to be discouraged from participating in the program. Medicaid participation was expected to be higher in states that offer a broad range of optional services, do not place arbitrary limits on the amounts of services covered, and extend eligibility to cover more categorically eligible and medically needy children.

12. Additionally, Held, et al. (1978) found: "The generosity of Medicaid reimbursement relative to area fees appears to be an important determinant of physician acceptance of Medicaid patients." Sloan and Steinwald (1978) obtained similar results in a study of Blue Shield participation. That is, an increase in the fee schedule for hospital visits is expected to increase participation by physicians. Also, in areas where Blue Shield has a high market share, physician participation appears to be higher. In a similar vein, Rice (1984) found that assignment rates under Medicare were sensitive to the reimbursement rate and, furthermore, that the assignment rates for ancillary services (laboratory and X-ray) are affected by changes in the reimbursement rate for medical services. Gabel and Rice (in press) synthesize the research findings from six studies on the changes in payment levels and conclude, "there appears to be a direct relationship between changes in physician payments under public programs, and physicians' willingness to participate in them.

13. In a production function context, the direction of causality is unclear, whether consistent use of preventive services leads to good health or whether those in good health have a propensity to use preventive services.

Chapter 3

RESEARCH DESIGN

The nature of the impact of Medicaid coverage on pediatric utilization is an empirical question. The purpose of this study is to assess the determinants of utilization among low-income children, with a special emphasis on the consequences of Medicaid eligibility. This study is designed to correct for some of the deficiencies in previous research.

The analysis is carried out in three phases: (1) profile of low-income children on Medicaid versus those not on Medicaid, with respect to socioeconomic characteristics and utilization patterns (Chapter 4); (2) assessment of the relative importance of a variety of factors on multiple indices of utilization, particularly the independent effect of Medicaid once other variables are controlled for (Chapter 5); and (3) display of predicted utilization measures (controlling for factors known to affect use) for low-income children, according to their health status and Medicaid coverage (Chapter 5).

The specific research questions to be answered by this study are listed below. Subsequent sections of this chapter describe the data base, the sample, the dependent and independent variables, the construction of the analysis file, and the implications of the complex survey design.

RESEARCH QUESTIONS

The research questions correspond to the three analytic phases of the study.

Phase I - Descriptive Analysis

1. What were the characteristics (in 1980) of the low-income children on Medicaid versus those not on Medicaid with respect to:

a. selected predisposing, enabling, and need factors associated
    with utilization; and

b. actual levels of utilization, unadjusted and crosstabulated
    with selected correlates of utilization.

Phase II - Regression Analysis

2. For each of the utilization indices, what are the significant
    determinants of utilization among low-income children?   In
    particular, what is the relative importance of Medicaid
    coverage?

3. For each of the utilization indices, what are the significant
    determinants of utilization for the Medicaid and non-Medicaid
    children considered separately? How are they similar? How do
    they differ?

4. What can be learned about the utilization patterns of low-
    income children by differentiating utilization according to (a)
    visits to physicians in office-based practice and (b) visits to
    physicians, regardless of setting?

5. What differences, if any, are demonstrated in the determinants
    of overall physician use versus preventive care use?

Phase III - Predictive Analysis

6. For each of the utilization indices, what is the annual predicted
    utilization by low-income children according to Medicaid
    coverage and health status?

OVERVIEW OF THE DATA BASE

This study uses data from the National Medical Care Utilization and
Expenditure Survey (NMCUES), a panel study of the U.S. noninstitutionalized
civilian population in 1980. NMCUES was designed to gather data on health
status, accessibility and utilization of health services, charges and sources of
payment associated with utilization, and the extent of health insurance
coverage in the population. The data collection was cosponsored by the
National Center for Health Statistics and the Health Care Financing
Administration, U.S. Department of Health and Human Services.

NMCUES emphasizes three major concerns of the sponsoring agencies (Bonham, 1983). One special purpose is to establish a data base for analyzing the characteristics of Medicaid recipients. Data on Medicaid eligibility have been verified against state administrative records. Another emphasis is the coverage and effectiveness of the Medicare program. For the first time, population-based data are available about elderly and disabled persons not covered by Medicare, services not paid for by Medicare, as well as characteristics of Medicare beneficiaries. The third special emphasis is on improving the reporting of mental health visits, as well as visits to hospital outpatient departments and hospital emergency rooms. Because previous surveys were believed to have undercounted these types of visits, special questions and probes were designed to improve the reporting of such visits.

The NMCUES survey design included three components. The National Household Survey (HHS) consists of 17,123 persons from about 6,000 randomly selected households. Each household was interviewed five times during 1980 and early 1981, roughly every three months. The State Medicaid Household Survey (SMHS) consists of 1,000 households selected from the 1979 Medicaid eligibility files in each of four states (California, Michigan, New York, and Texas). The same survey form and data collection procedures were used for both the HHS and SMHS samples. Finally, the Administrative Records Survey (ARS) verified selected Medicaid and Medicare data collected in the two household surveys (HHS and SMHS) with data contained in the federal Medicare file and the state Medicaid file.

The present study is based on data gathered in the National Household Survey. This data source is well-suited for the purposes of the study because of the emphases on verifying Medicaid eligibility and on measuring visits to hospital outpatient departments and emergency rooms. Additionally, because the NMCUES is a panel study with five rounds of interviews, respondent recall is enhanced. Another advantage is that data on income are reported concurrently with health service use, rather than for a prior time period.

Appendix 2 provides additional detail on the sampling, interview, weighting, and imputation procedures employed in the HHS component.

SAMPLE SELECTION

A subsample of children was selected from the NMCUES sample, including those under age 18 living in families with incomes below 150 percent of the federal poverty level. This study differs from previous studies in the population of inference. Most importantly, the data are national in scope, permitting generalizations to the U.S. population. Second, the study sample is restricted to children in low-income families, rather than including children of all incomes. Thus, the study sample more closely resembles the target population for governmental initiatives. Another difference is that this study includes adolescents, a group that was frequently overlooked in previous research.

The selection criteria were as follows:

1. Only children under age 18, as of January 1, 1980, were included in the study.

2. Only children living in families with family income in 1980 below 150 percent of the federal poverty threshold were included. This criterion limits the sample to poor and near poor children and is the same poverty cut-off used by Gortmaker (1981) and the Robert Wood Johnson Foundation (1983). The poverty level is based on family income adjusted for family size as well as age and sex of household head.[1]

3. Only children who were eligible for the survey for the entire survey period were included. This criterion excludes those children who were born or who died during 1980, as well as those who were institutionalized for part of the year.

Of the 5,074 children ages 0 through 17 who were eligible for NMCUES for the entire survey period, 1,409 were living below 150 percent of the federal poverty level. Of the 1,409 children, 484 had Medicaid coverage for the full year. Table 1 displays the number of children (unweighted) in the study sample according to Medicaid coverage and poverty level.

The population of inference has one major limitation. As noted above, only children who were eligible for the survey the entire year are included in the study sample. Clearly, the children who have been excluded-- those who were born, who died, or who were institutionalized in 1980--tend to be high users of medical care. In spite of this restriction, newborn care is accounted for, to some extent, in the children who were born in 1979 (n = 83). Furthermore, the numbers of low-income children who died (n = 1) or were institutionalized (n = 4) in 1980 are so small that they preclude meaningful and reliable analysis of these events. On a more technical level, this restriction simplified the calculation of means and variances. Only children for whom the "basic person weight" is equal to the "time-adjusted person weight" are included in the study sample. (Refer to Appendix 2 for more details on the weighting procedures in NMCUES.)

TABLE 1

UNWEIGHTED NUMBER OF LOW-INCOME CHILDREN IN THE
NMCUES SAMPLE, ACCORDING TO MEDICAID COVERAGE AND
POVERTY STATUS

		MEDICAID COVERAGE		
Poverty Level	Total	Full year	Part year	None
Total below 150% of poverty level	1,409	529	125	755
Below poverty level	825	427	78	320
1.00–1.24% of poverty level	268	56	20	192
1.25–1.49% of poverty level	316	46	27	243

Source: 1980 National Medical Care Utilization and Expenditure Survey.

SPECIFICATION OF THE MODEL:
DEPENDENT VARIABLES

This study uses multiple utilization indices to allow a comprehensive and systematic analysis of the effect of Medicaid, including measures of the probability and volume of physician visits as well as the probability of preventive care use. Each measure is repeated for office-based physician visits and physician visits regardless of setting (including services provided by nonphysicians under the supervision of a physician). (See Table 2.)

The means and standard errors for the six dependent variables are displayed in Table 3. It should be noted that the standard errors are relatively small, indicating that there is not a lot of variation on the dependent variables. In particular, for the two volume equations, most of the children were very low users: of the 997 children with at least one visit, 64 percent had one, two, or three visits. Only 8 percent had ten or more visits. As another example, the use of preventive care in 1980 was a relatively rare event, with 18 percent of the 1,409 children making a preventive visit. In such cases, predicting a relatively rare event tends to be difficult.

Appendix 3 provides documentation on the construction of the dependent variables. Several issues concerning the specification of the dependent variables are discussed below.

Probability of Contact Versus Volume of Visits

Separate analyses of the probability of use and the volume of visits are conducted for theoretical and statistical reasons. From a theoretical perspective, separate equations are desirable because they represent different behavioral processes. The probability equation reflects the decision to seek or not to seek care. As such, it permits an analysis of the factors associated with initiating contact. The volume equation captures another facet of decision-making--the decision to stop after one visit or to make multiple visits. This decision involves the provider as well as the patient. Different factors would be expected, *a priori*, to explain the probability versus the volume of use. (See, for example, Rossiter and Wilensky, 1983.)

Separate equations are also warranted on the basis of statistical considerations. The distribution of physician use (both aggregate and preventive use) is non-normal, due to two factors: (1) a concentration of nonusers with zero visits; and (2) a small number of high users. In such a case it is inappropriate to apply a linear regression model. A better approach is to treat the use/nonuse decision as a dichotomous choice (where use is assigned a value of one and nonuse is set equal to zero). The cumulative logistic

TABLE 2

DEFINITION OF THE DEPENDENT AND INDEPENDENT VARIABLES

I. Dependent Variables*

Variable Name	Definition
VSTALLMH	= 1, if child had at least one visit to MD or non-MD working with an MD
VSTPRVMH	= 1, if child had at least one visit to MD in private practice
PREVALL	= 1, if child had preventive checkup from MD or non-MD working with an MD
PREVPRIV	= 1, if child had preventive checkup from MD in private practice
LOGALLMH	Number of visits to MD or non-MD working with an MD, for children with at least one visit (log)
LOGPRVMH	Number of visits to MD in private practice, for children with at least one visit (log)

II. Independent Variables

Variable Name	Definition	Source**

A. Sociodemographic Characteristics

REALAGE	Age, as of January 1, 1980	P54
AGESQ	REALAGE-squared	P54
SEX1	= 1, if male; 0, if female (used only in PREVPRIV)	P59
RACE3	= 1, if nonwhite; 0, if white	P57
EDSTAT	= 1, if no family members graduated high school; 0, otherwise	F173, F176, F179, F182, F185, F188
CHILDREN	Number of children under age 17 in family and living in household	F164, F167

B. Economic Factors

INCOME	Family income annualized for 1980	P40

TABLE 2 (continued)

DEFINITION OF THE DEPENDENT AND INDEPENDENT VARIABLES

OOPPCT	Out-of-pocket payment for MD visits relative to the total charges for MD visits (used for LOGALLMH and LOGPRVMH equations only)	(P265 + P271 + P277 + P289 + P295)/(P193 + P199 + P205 + P217 + P223)
	Dummy variables for insurance coverage in 1980; Medicaid coverage omitted category***	
PRIVATE	=1, if covered only by private insurance during 1980; 0, otherwise	
UNINSURE	=1, if uninsured the entire year; 0, otherwise	
TRAVEL	Usual one-way travel time to regular source, in minutes (used in equations excluding children without a regular source)	P562
WAIT	Usual waiting time, in minutes (used in equations excluding children without a regular source of care)	P565

C. Organizational Variables

	Dummy variables for type of regular source of care; no regular source of care omitted category (used only in LOGALLMH and LOGPRVMH)	
RSMD	=1, if regular source of care is a physician's office; 0, otherwise	P553= 1 and P554 = 1 or 2
RSNONMD	=1, if regular source is other than a physician's office; 0, otherwise	P553 = 1 and P554 > 2

D. Community Resource Variables

PC_MD	Ratio of office-based, patient care physicians engaged in primary care, per 100,000 persons in the county (primary care includes family/general practitioners, pediatricians, and obstetrician/gynecologists)	Area Resource File
RATIOGP	Relative fee within states for general practitoners under Medicaid and Medicare	Holahan, 1984

TABLE 2 (continued)

DEFINITION OF THE DEPENDENT AND INDEPENDENT VARIABLES

ERLAND	Number of hospital emergency rooms in the county per 100,000 square miles in the county	Area Resource File

E. Health Status Measures

PHS_LIM	=1, if perceived health status fair or poor or if some limitation in activity	P67 = 3 or 4, or P66 < 4
BEDDAYL	Number of bed disability days in 1980 (log)	P125
HOSP	=1, if hospitalization in 1980	P167 > 0

*The construction and source of the dependent variables is discussed in Appendix 3.

**The alphanumeric variable label indicates the file name and beginning file position for the variable, as listed in the NMCUES Public Use Data Tape Documentation (NCHS, 1983c). The file names are referred to as follows: P - person file, F - family file, and M - medical visit file.

***Refer to Appendix 4 for additional details on the construction of the insurance measures.

TABLE 3

WEIGHTED MEANS AND STANDARD ERRORS FOR THE STUDY SAMPLE*

Variable Name	Brief Description	Mean	Standard Error
VSTALLMH	Probability of visit	0.710	0.017
VSTPRVMH	Probability of visit to private MD	0.478	0.019
LOGALLMH	Number of visits (log)	0.982	0.035
LOGPRVMH	Number of visits to private MD	0.693	0.029
PREVALL	Probability of preventive visit	0.175	0.014
PREVPRIV	Probability of preventive visit to private MD	0.091	0.011
REALAGE	Age at beginning of 1980	7.969	0.203
AGESQ	Age-squared	90.209	3.181
SEX1	Sex	0.503	0.015
RACE3	Race	0.335	0.031
EDSTAT	Educational status of family	0.410	0.029
CHILDREN	Number of children in family	3.144	0.100
INCOME	Family income in 1980	8700.397	272.069
OOPPCT**	Percent paid out-of-pocket	3.761	0.317
PRIVATE	Private health insurance coverage	0.381	0.027
UNINSURE	No insurance coverage the entire year	0.160	0.017
RSMD	Regular source is MD office	0.523	0.026
RSNONMD	Regular source is not MD office	0.326	0.026
TRAVEL***	Travel time to regular source	18.084	0.825
WAIT***	Waiting time at regular source	43.012	3.113
PC_MD	Primary care physician rate	383.909	22.716
RATIOGP	MCAID/MCARE fee for GPs	0.741	0.016
ERLAND	ERs per 100,000 square miles	72.596	11.105
PHS_LIM	Perceived health/activity limitation	0.095	0.010
BEDDAYL	Number of bed days (log)	0.959	0.040
HOSP	Hospitalized in 1980	0.078	0.008

*The means and standard errors were generated by PROC SURREGR under SAS. These measures take into account the complex sample design. Refer to Table 4 for information on variable coding.

**Includes only children with at least one physician visit.

***Includes only children with a regular source of care.

Source: 1980 National Medical Care Utilization and Expenditure Survey.

probability function predicts the probability of seeking care within the (0,1) range.

The volume equations are handled by weighted least squares regression, since the dependent variables are continuous measures. Because of the non-normal distribution of visits among users, the volume measures are log-transformed.

Probability of Overall Physician Use Versus Preventive Use

A separate set of equations is specified for the probability of preventive care use. This is desirable for three reasons. The first is theoretical. Colle and Grossman (1978) suggest that preventive and curative visits are separate inputs into the production of health and furthermore, that these visits produce different outputs. The second rationale is based on empirical evidence. Berki and Ashcraft (1979) conducted research on the utilization experience of 626 families employed by a single firm in Rochester, New York. They found that different factors explained the use of preventive services compared to illness-related services. The third reason is based on standards of pediatric practice. The American Academy of Pediatrics' Standards of Child Health Care (1977) recommends a schedule of health supervision visits throughout the infancy, preschool, and schoolage periods. However, the Academy has acknowledged that the Standards are not based on empirical evidence of the effect of health supervision (except immunization) on the health of children and youth.

Expenditures Versus Visits in Measuring Utilization

This study uses "visits" rather than expenditures as the unit of measurement of the dependent variables. Manning, Newhouse, and Ware (1982) reported that, according to their estimates, "expenditures and visits are highly correlated." Andersen and Benham (1970) studied the relationship between use and income and found that expenditures significantly underestimated the services consumed by the poor, due to the use of free and subsidized care.

Another rationale is provided by unpublished research by Anderson and Thorne (1984). Based on data from the National Medical Care Utilization and Expenditure Survey, they found "underreporting by NMCUES households of government expenditures on their behalf." However, the authors concluded that "NMCUES accurately estimated utilization of health services, if not per service cost."

Physician Office Visits Versus Aggregate Physician Visits

The distinction between physician office visits and aggregate visits (regardless of setting) is being made because the effect of Medicaid on health service use is expected to vary depending on the type of contact. As discussed previously, Colle and Grossman (1978) found that preschool children receiving welfare (and Medicaid) had a higher likelihood of a preventive exam or any type of physician contact, compared to children not on welfare. However, the number of office visits to physicians in private practice, and particularly specialists, was negatively associated with Medicaid coverage. Wolfe (1981) arrived at similar findings for a sample of children from Rochester, New York.

SPECIFICATION OF THE MODEL:
INDEPENDENT VARIABLES

The independent variables represent the hypothesized determinants of physician use. They are grouped in five categories: sociodemographic characteristics; economic factors; organizational variables; community resources; and health status measures. Table 2 defines the independent variables used in the analyses. Table 3 displays descriptive statistics for each independent variable.

The first group of independent variables, sociodemographic characteristics, is relatively straightforward. Actual age (REALAGE) and the quadratic age term (AGESQ) are both included to capture the hypothesized nonlinear effects of age. Other sociodemographic characteristics included in the model are race (RACE3), number of children in the family (CHILDREN), and educational level of the family (EDSTAT). EDSTAT is based on all family members age 17 and over, and reflects the educational status of the member with the highest educational level.

In addition, sex (SEX1) is controlled in the equation for the probability of a preventive office visit (PREVPRIV) because adolescent females tend to have higher use of private physicians for fertility-related services. Otherwise, no differential effects according to sex would be expected, and this was confirmed by preliminary analyses.

Income is measured by actual (reported) income in 1980 (INCOME). As income increases, use is expected to decrease. Money price is measured by the out-of-pocket charge relative to the total charge for physician visits (OOPPCT). For those with zero visits, however, out-of-pocket costs will automatically be equal to zero. Because of the sizable proportion of nonusers, this measure is not appropriate for the analyses of probability of use. Thus,

OOPPCT is restricted to the volume equations (LOGALLMH and LOGPRVMH).

The probability equations (VSTALLMH, VSTPRVMH, PREVALL, PREVPRIV) control for the type of insurance as a measure of the effect of third-party coverage. However, insurance coverage is complicated to measure in a longitudinal survey due to changes over the course of the year. Two dummy variables are used in this study: private insurance for all or part of the year and no Medicaid coverage during the year (PRIVATE); and no insurance coverage during the entire year (UNINSURE). The omitted category is Medicaid coverage during all or part of the year. Thus, the coefficients on the insurance variables reflect the difference between the specified type of coverage and Medicaid coverage (as measured by the intercept). Appendix 4 describes the assumptions and methods used to derive these measures of insurance coverage.

Time costs are operationalized by measures of the amount of time spent traveling to a regular source of care (TRAVEL) and waiting to see the provider (WAIT). Because values are available only for those reporting a regular source of care, TRAVEL and WAIT are used only in the analyses concerning those with a regular source of care.

The type of regular source may be associated with a variety of organizational barriers or incentives. However, those with no regular source probably face greater information and search costs than those with any type of regular source. Having a regular source of care is frequently related to previous use of health care; that is, high users are more likely to report a regular source than low users or nonusers. For this reason, the probability equations do not control for whether the child had a regular source of care. The volume equations, however do contain a measure of the type of regular source, to test the effect of a regular source on the number of visits among those with at least one. A distinction is made between a physician's office as the regular source of care (RSMD) and all other types of regular sources (RSNONMD). No regular source of care is the omitted category. Because the number of children with a regular source other than a physician's office is small, it is not possible to analyze the independent effects of these other types (e.g., emergency room, hospital outpatient department, health clinic).

As discussed in the previous chapter, supply characteristics are rarely significant in person-level analyses. Preliminary analyses tested a wide range of "community resource" proxies and arrived at a parsimonious set of variables.[2] A measure of aggregate physician stock is specified--the ratio of office-based, patient care physicians engaged in primary care, per 100,000 persons in the child's county of residence (PC_MD). Primary care physicians include family/general practitioners, pediatricians, and obstetricians/ gynecologists. In addition, because this study focuses on low-income children, two measures are included that reflect the health resources frequently used by this population. One indicates the availability of emergency rooms in terms of the county's land area (ERLAND). The second is the relative reimbursement level within states under Medicaid and Medicare for a general practitioner (RATIOGP).[3] The fee ratio, according to Holahan (1982), "give(s) a good approximation of the differences between Medicaid and average price charges."[4]

Three measures of health status are specified, including a combined measure of perceived health status and activity limitation at the beginning of the year (PHS_LIM) and the number of bed days during the year (BEDDAYL). In addition, a hospitalization (HOSP) during 1980 is expected to be associated with more ambulatory care.

CONSTRUCTION OF THE ANALYSIS FILE

Prior to engaging in the descriptive and multivariate analyses, the analysis file was created. This involved applying the sampling criteria discussed previously and then linking the child's personal data with data from other sources. In addition, variables were recoded as necessary, log transformations were performed on variables with non-normal distributions, and outliers were evaluated. The remainder of this section discusses the seven data sources that contributed to the analysis file.

The NMCUES person file on the public use tape formed the "backbone" of the analysis file.[5] The sampling criteria were applied to this file and all subsequent linkages were made to the resulting file. The NMCUES person file contributed the majority of the data for the independent variables and selected items for the dependent variables.

In the next phase of file construction, the public use data on medical visits were linked with the child's personal data. Because the NMCUES medical visit file contains one record per visit, it was necessary to aggregate the visit records for each child (using PROC SUMMARY under SAS). The aggregated visit data were then merged with the child's personal data. Children with no medical visits during the year had no visit records, and thus, the merge produced "missing data" for those with zero visits. The missing data were recoded to zeroes.

The third linkage involved family level data from the NMCUES family analysis tape (Moser et al. 1984). The merge was based on the encrypted family identification code; where there was more than one child per family, identical family data were attached to each child's record.

In the next phase, each child's record was linked to a file containing confidential identifiers of the child's state and county of residence, as represented by the Federal Information Processing (FIP) codes. These identifiers facilitated the linkage of area data from the three remaining sources. One source was the Area Resource File, containing county level data on physician (MDs and DOs) distribution from the American Medical Association, hospital resource data from the American Hospital Association, and 1980 Census population figures (ODAM, 1984). In addition, state-level information on reimbursement of physicians under Medicaid and Medicare (Holahan, 1984) and state data on Medicaid eligibility criteria (Muse and Sawyer, 1982) were linked to each child's record. Data from these last two sources were not automated, so they were first entered into separate files and then merged with the child's personal data.

IMPLICATIONS OF THE
COMPLEX SURVEY DESIGN

The complex stratified multistage probability sample design used in the NMCUES has major implications for this study's research design. The data analysis must take the complex survey design into account by adjusting for both the sampling weights and the design features. Variance estimation, in particular, is more complicated using complex survey data. It is inappropriate to use statistical procedures that assume simple random sampling because of clustering, stratification, and unequal probabilities of selection. Standard methods based on simple random sampling assumptions tend to underestimate the true variance. Cohen and Kalsbeek (1978) describe the effect of design features on inferences from regression models:

> The variances of the regression coefficients generated by ordinary least squares are generally under-estimated by assuming simple random sampling. This will have the effect of producing F-statistics that are too large too often, suggesting that too many significant results could be expected. . .

To allow for "design-based inference," the strategy recommended by Landis et al. (1982) has been adapted. First, all preliminary hypotheses were tested without regard to the design features and without the sampling weights. In the second stage, the sample weights and design effects were taken into account. This stage involved a more rigorous analysis of (1) significant results obtained in the first stage, and (2) relationships that were not significant but thought to be substantively important.

Three approaches have been developed to estimate variances for surveys with complex survey designs: balance repeated replication (BRR), the jackknife method, and Taylor series approximation. All rely on the same assumptions concerning sample design and all give comparable results.

However, computer software is readily available only for the BRR and Taylor series approaches. This study used the Taylor series approach for two reasons. First, it is more efficient computationally; and second, it runs under SAS.

The variances were estimated using computer software developed at Research Triangle Institute and run under SAS. The SESUDAAN program (Shah, 1981) produces standard errors for means, totals, and proportions. The SURREGR program (Shah, 1982) handles regressions with continuous dependent variables, generating weighted regression coefficients as well as standard errors.

The standard errors in logistic regressions were adjusted using a method employed by researchers at the National Center for Health Services Research (Cohen and Gridley, 1981). The method is as follows: (1) the model was run with weighted least squares, to obtain the variance estimate under simple random sampling assumptions; (2) the model was run with SURREGR, to obtain the variance estimate under the complex sample design; (3) the design effect was derived by dividing the second variance estimate by the first; (4) the standard error obtained under logistic regression was adjusted by the square-root of the design effect, except that design effects less than one were ignored; and (5) the new t-value was derived by dividing the coefficient by the adjusted standard error.

Appendix 5 illustrates the effect of the complex sample design on the regression coefficients and the estimates of the standard errors. All regression estimates presented in Chapter 5 are adjusted for the complex sample design.

NOTES

1. The 1980 federal poverty thresholds used in the NMCUES were as follows:

POVERTY LEVEL

Average Number of persons in family	Age of Head	Male Head	Female Head
1.0 - 1.4	Under 65	$4,441	$4,109
	65 and over	3,990	3,938
1.5 - 2.4	Under 65	5,568	5,415
	65 and over	4,988	4,946
2.5 - 3.4		6,608	6,386
3.5 - 4.4		8,418	8,382
4.5 - 5.4		9,976	9,878
5.5 - 6.4		11,274	11,227
6.5 or more		13,986	13,767

The cut-offs for the sample are 1.5 times the poverty thresholds above.

2. Preliminary regression analyses tested several alternate specifications of the community resource variables. For example, early analyses included geographic indicators for region and residence (i.e., residence in the South and SMSA/non-SMSA residence). These variables were eliminated because no significant effects were found when the provider availability measures were controlled.

In addition, three other aggregate physician supply variables were tested (along with the associated Medicaid physician participation variables): (1) the ratio of office-based, patient care pediatricians per 1,000 children ages 0 through 18; (2) the ratio of non-pediatricians in office-based, patient care practice per 10,000 persons (all ages) in the county; and (3) the ratio of office-based, patient care pediatricians and general practitioners (weighted by 0.25) per 100,000 children ages 0 through 18. These three variables did not perform as well as the primary care physician ratio (PC_MD).

Besides the aggregate physician supply variable (PC_MD) and the relative fee variable (RATIOGP), an interaction term was constructed by multiplying PC_MD and RATIOGP. The resulting variable was designed as a proxy for the level of Medicaid participation among primary care physicians.

Because the interaction was highly correlated with PC_MD, a decision was made to drop the interaction term and retain the original variables.

Finally, a measure of the availability of hospital outpatient departments was tested in preliminary analyses and eliminated because of its nonsignificant effect.

3. Other proxies for the acceptance of Medicaid recipients may be preferable, such as the percent of physicians' patient load consisting of Medicaid patients; and the percent of physicians accepting new Medicaid patients. Such measures have been employed by Held et al. (1978) and Davidson et al. (1980). However, these measures were not available for all jurisdictions in the United States.

4. Regression analyses involving RATIOGP have excluded the children living in Arizona because there was no Medicaid program in that state in 1980. There is no real or imputable value for Arizona's fee ratio.

5. The NMCUES public use tape (NCHS, 1983c) contains six files: person, medical visit, hospital stay, dental visit, prescribed medicines and other expenses, and conditions. Data from the first two files only were used in this study. Additionally, the NMCUES family analysis tape provided the family-level data (Moser et al., 1984).

Chapter 4

PROFILE OF LOW-INCOME CHILDREN

This chapter describes the population of low-income children in terms of their health insurance coverage, health service use, and expenditures for health care. The first section compares the insurance coverage of low-income children to that of children of all incomes. Next, the characteristics of low-income children covered by Medicaid versus those not on Medicaid are examined. Finally, an overview is presented on the use of and expenditures for physicians' services, according to type of coverage. The data presented in this chapter are weighted estimates for the noninstitutionalized, civilian population in the United States, as defined in Chapter 3.

OVERVIEW OF INSURANCE COVERAGE

Of the 63.9 million children under age 18 in the United States in 1980, about one-fourth (16.8 million) lived in poor and near-poor families (defined as families with incomes below 150 percent of the federal poverty level).[1] Nearly one-half (46 percent) of the 16.8 million low-income children were covered by Medicaid for all or part of 1980, including 31 percent covered by Medicaid only for the full year; 3 percent covered by Medicaid for part of 1980 and uninsured for the remainder of the year; and 12 percent covered by both Medicaid and private insurance during the year. (See Table 4.)

An additional 30 percent of the low-income children were privately insured for the full year, while 8 percent had private insurance coverage for part of the year and were uninsured otherwise. Sixteen percent of the children in low-income families, or 2.7 million children, were uninsured for all of 1980. When added to the 3 percent with part year Medicaid coverage and the 8 percent with private coverage part of the year, over one-fourth (28 percent) were uninsured for at least part of 1980. This figure is almost twice as high as the percent of nonpoor children uninsured for at least part of the year (15 percent).

TABLE 4

INSURANCE COVERAGE OF CHILDREN IN 1980, BY POVERTY STATUS*

Type of Insurance Coverage	ALL CHILDREN		LOW-INCOME CHILDREN		NONPOOR CHILDREN	
	Number (in 000s)	Percent of Children	Number (in 000s)	Percent of Children	Number (in 000s)	Percent of Children
Total	63,871	100.0	16,846	100.0	47,026	100.0
Medicaid Coverage	10,855	17.0	7,726	45.9	3,129	6.7
Full year	6,494	10.2	5,264	31.2	1,230	2.6
Part year	973	1.5	515	3.1	458	1.0
With private ins.	3,388	5.3	1,947	11.6	1,441	3.1
Private Insurance	47,276	74.0	6,425	38.1	40,851	86.9
Full year	42,532	66.6	5,011	29.7	37,521	79.8
Part year	4,744	7.4	1,414	8.4	3,330	7.1
No Insurance in 1980	5,740	9.0	2,695	16.0	3,045	6.5

*Low–income children live in families with incomes below 150 percent of the federal poverty level. Nonpoor children live in families with incomes at or above 150 percent of the federal poverty level.

Source: 1980 National Medical Care Utilization and Expenditure Survey.

As expected, the predominant form of insurance coverage among nonpoor children is private insurance: 80 percent were covered the full year, 7 percent part of the year, and 3 percent in combination with Medicaid coverage.

CRITERIA FOR MEDICAID ELIGIBILITY

Medicaid eligibility is based on a variety of financial and categorical criteria. All states must provide Medicaid coverage to children in families receiving Aid to Families with Dependent Children (AFDC). However, there is considerable variation among states in the financial criteria because states determine the payment standards upon which AFDC eligibility is based. The level of a state's payment standard reflects its fiscal capabilities and attitudes towards assisting the poor (Rymer et al. 1979). AFDC is targeted to children in single-parent families, although 25 states and the District of Columbia provided AFDC (as well as Medicaid) to children in two-parent families with an unemployed parent in 1980. (See Table 5.) In addition, 29 states and the District of Columbia provided Medicaid coverage to children in two-parent families that did not meet the categorical requirements of AFDC, but did meet the financial criteria (Muse and Sawyer, 1982).

Another optional group, covered by 29 states and the District of Columbia, is the "medically needy." This group is comprised of those who did not qualify financially for public assistance (AFDC), but whose medical expenses enabled them to "spend down" their income to qualify for Medicaid. Blind and disabled children receiving Supplemental Security Income (SSI) were automatically covered by Medicaid in 33 states and the District of Columbia; the remaining 17 states placed some restrictions on Medicaid coverage of SSI recipients (Muse and Sawyer, 1982).

Gaps exist in Medicaid coverage of children within states that do not cover one or more of the optional groups discussed above. In addition, states with very low AFDC payment standards exclude low-income children in single-parent families whose income exceeds the financial limit, but is still below the poverty level.

CHARACTERISTICS OF LOW-INCOME
CHILDREN ACCORDING TO
INSURANCE COVERAGE

This analysis is designed to provide a profile of low-income children according to Medicaid coverage and selected socioeconomic and health status characteristics. Because of the emphasis in this analysis on comparing

TABLE 5

ELIGIBILITY CRITERIA FOR STATE MEDICAID PROGRAMS, DECEMBER 1980

State	Families with unemployed parent covered by AFDC	Poor children in two-parent families not on AFDC	Medically needy	All SSI recipients
Total	26	30	30	34
Alabama	--	X	--	X
Alaska	--	--	--	X
Arizona*	--	--	--	--
Arkansas	--	X	X	X
California	X	X	X	X
Colorado	X	--	--	X
Connecticut	X	X	X	--
Delaware	X	--	--	X
District of Columbia	X	X	X	X
Florida	--	--	--	X
Georgia	--	X	--	X
Hawaii	X	X	X	--
Idaho	--	X	--	X
Illinois	X	--	X	--
Indiana	--	--	--	--
Iowa	X	--	--	X

TABLE 5 (continued)

ELIGIBILITY CRITERIA FOR STATE MEDICAID PROGRAMS, DECEMBER 1980

State	Families with unemployed parent covered by AFDC	Poor children in two-parent families not on AFDC	Medically needy	All SSI recipients
Kansas	X	--	X	X
Kentucky	--	X	X	X
Louisiana	--	X	X	X
Maine	--	X	X	X
Maryland	X	X	X	X
Massachusetts	X	X	X	X
Michigan	X	X	X	X
Minnesota	X	X	X	--
Mississippi	--	--	--	--
Missouri	X	--	--	--
Montana	X	X	X	X
Nebraska	X	--	X	--
Nevada	--	X	--	X
New Hampshire	--	X	X	--
New Jersey	X	X	--	X
New Mexico	--	--	--	X
New York	X	--	X	--
North Carolina	--	--	X	--
North Dakota	--	X	X	--

TABLE 5 (continued)

ELIGIBILITY CRITERIA FOR STATE MEDICAID PROGRAMS, DECEMBER 1980

State	Families with unemployed parent covered by AFDC	Poor children in two-parent families not on AFDC	Medically needy	All SSI recipients
Ohio	X	--	--	--
Oklahoma	--	X	X	--
Oregon	--	X	--	X
Pennsylvania	X	X	X	X
Rhode Island	X	X	X	X
South Carolina	--	X	--	X
South Dakota	--	--	--	X
Tennessee	--	X	X	X
Texas	--	--	--	X
Utah	X	X	X	--
Vermont	X	X	X	X
Virginia	--	--	X	--
Washington	X	X	X	X
West Virginia	X	--	X	X
Wisconsin	X	X	X	X
Wyoming	--	--	--	X

X = covergage offered by the state; -- = coverage not offered by the state.
*As of December 1980, Arizona did not have a Medicaid program.

Note: See text for description of eligiblity criteria.

Source: Muse and Sawyer, 1982.

Medicaid and non-Medicaid children, insurance coverage is categorized as shown in Table 6. These figures are comparable to those presented in Table 4 with two modifications: (1) children receiving both Medicaid and private insurance in 1980 have been classified in the "full year" and "part year" Medicaid categories regardless of their private insurance coverage (the total with Medicaid is unchanged, however); and (2) the separate full year and part year private insurance categories have been collapsed into one category. These regroupings preserve the distinctions between the insured and uninsured children as well as between full year and part year Medicaid recipients, while maintaining cell sizes sufficient for analysis.

The comparative analysis that follows is based on 12 variables that are hypothesized to affect Medicaid eligibility. (See Figure 2.) These hypotheses were tested (via t-tests) by comparing the characteristics of Medicaid and non-Medicaid children (columns 3 and 6 in Table 6). Unless otherwise stated, only statistically significant differences ($p < 0.5$) are discussed in the text.

As shown in Table 6, Medicaid and non-Medicaid children did not differ significantly in age; the average age was roughly 8 years in both groups. Also, there were no statistical differences between the two groups with respect to the proportion of females.

The type of coverage for blacks and whites was significantly different, with black children accounting for 45 percent of the low-income children covered by Medicaid the full year, 20 percent of the uninsured, and 21 percent of the privately insured. (Overall, black children comprised 30 percent of the low-income children.) The lower level of Medicaid coverage and higher level of no insurance among white children may be due, in part, to the fact that a higher proportion of white children were living in two-parent families compared to black children. As discussed previously, AFDC (and hence, Medicaid) is targeted to children in single-parent families, although 30 states extend Medicaid to children in two-parent families. (The small number of children of other races and the unreliability of the estimates preclude any separate discussion of this subpopulation).

Half of the children on Medicaid the full year or uninsured the full year lived in families where no adult had graduated from high school. A significantly lower proportion (about one-fourth) of the children covered by private insurance lived in families with no high school graduate. Educational status may be associated with a parent's employment status or place of employment, and hence, insurance coverage.

As expected from the Medicaid eligibility criteria, children covered by Medicaid either full year or part year were significantly more likely to be living in single-parent families (72 percent) than those not on Medicaid (25 percent). Both Medicaid and non-Medicaid children lived in families with an average of three children in the household.

TABLE 6

CHARACTERISTICS OF LOW-INCOME CHILDREN, ACCORDING TO INSURANCE COVERAGE, 1980

Characteristic	Low-income Children	Total Medicaid	Medicaid Full Year	Medicaid Part Year	Total non-Medicaid	Privately Insured	Uninsured
Number of children (000s)	16,846	7,726	6,248	1,478	9,120	6,425	2,695
Percent of total	100.0	45.9	37.1	8.8	54.1	38.1	16.0
Average age (years)	8.0	7.7	7.5	8.7	8.2	8.3	7.9
Percent female	49.7	48.6	47.9	51.3	50.7	49.3	54.1
Percent black	30.3	41.9	45.2	27.7	20.5	20.8	19.9
Percent no high school graduate in family	41.0	48.4	50.8	38.4	34.7	27.1	52.8
Percent single–parent families	46.5	72.2	72.8	70.0	24.8	22.0	31.4
Average number of children	3.1	3.2	3.2	3.0	3.1	3.2	3.0
Average income	$8,700	$7,138	$6,907	$8,117	$10,024	$10,318	$9,323
Percent below poverty	58.2	76.2	79.0	64.7	42.9	41.2	47.0
Percent living in South	34.9	27.6	25.7	35.4	41.2	40.8	42.2
Percent in fair/poor health or with activity limit	9.5	11.7	11.1	14.2	7.6	6.7	9.7
Percent hospitalized in 1980	7.8	10.4	9.4	13.4	5.9	7.2	2.6
Average number of bed–days	3.9	4.0	3.9	4.7	3.7	3.8	3.4

Source: 1980 National Medical Care Utilization and Expenditure Survey.

FIGURE 2

VARIABLES INCLUDED IN THE DESCRIPTIVE ANALYSIS
OF MEDICAID AND NON-MEDICAID CHILDREN

Selected Variables*	Hypothesized relationship to Medicaid eligiblity
Age	Younger children (under age 6) are expected to be more likely to receive AFDC and thus Medicaid because their mothers are less likely to be employed outside the home. (-)
Sex	No hypothesized relationship, except pregnant adolescents and adolescent mothers may be covered by Medicaid. (?)
Race	Black children are expected to be more likely to have Medicaid coverage because their average family income is lower than that of white children. (+)
Education	Children in families with no high school graduates are expected to be more likely to receive AFDC and Medicaid because of possible associations among education, employment, and income, thus increasing the likelihood of financial eligiblity for public assistance. (-)
Family Structure	Children in single-parent families are expected to be more likely to have Medicaid coverage because of AFDC's categorical eligiblity requirements and because only 30 states provide Medicaid coverage to poor children in two-parent families. (-)
Number of Children	Children in large families are expected to be more likely to have Medicaid coverage because of lower per capita income. (+)
Income	Children in lower-income families are expected to be more likely to have Medicaid coverage than those in higher-income families because of financial criteria for Medicaid eligibility. (-)
Poverty Level	As hypothesized for income, children below the federal poverty level are expected to be more likely to have Medicaid coverage than those above poverty. (-)
Residence in the South	Children living outside the South are expected to be more likely to have Medicaid coverage than those residing in the South because of the lower AFDC income eligibility level and the coverage of fewer optional categories by Southern states. (-)

Self-reported Health Status	Children in fair/poor health or with an activity limitation are expected to be more likely to have Medicaid coverage because of the medically needy eligiblity criteria in 30 states, and perhaps because of financial eligiblity for AFDC if the mother is unable to work outside the home while caring for a child with a disability. (+)
Hospitalization	Children who were hospitalized are expected to be more likely to have Medicaid coverage because of the "spend-down" provisions in states that cover the medically needy. (+)
Number of Bed Days	As with health status above, children with more bed days are expected to be more likely to have Medicaid coverage. (+)

*See Chapter 3, Research Design for additional information on variable definitions and coding.

Low-income children covered by Medicaid lived in families with an average income of $7,138. This was significantly lower than the average family income of non-Medicaid children ($10,024). Children on Medicaid the full year had the lowest family income on average ($6,907), while the privately insured had the highest ($10,318).

Restrictive financial and categorical criteria clearly prevented some of the uninsured population from qualifying for Medicaid: about half of the uninsured children lived in families below poverty. The remaining half of the uninsured were near-poor (100 to 150 percent of poverty). As would be expected, three-fourths of the Medicaid children were below poverty.

Low-income children living in the South represented 35 percent of the total, but only 28 percent of those covered by Medicaid for all or part of the year. Children in the South accounted for a disproportionate share of the non-Medicaid population (both the uninsured and privately insured). Southern states tend to have lower income eligibility criteria for AFDC and, as a result, provide public assistance to a smaller proportion of the children in poverty (Kovar and Meny, 1980).

Of the low-income children on Medicaid for all or part of the year, 12 percent were in fair or poor health or had an activity limitation, compared to 8 percent of the non-Medicaid children. A significantly higher proportion of the Medicaid children were hospitalized in 1980. Both groups had roughly the same number of bed-days on average.

It would appear that low-income children who were covered by Medicaid part year may be in poorer health than other children, as indicated by the percent hospitalized in 1980. It should be noted however, that a causal relationship among health status, health service use, and Medicaid coverage is likely. Children in poor health who have high medical care costs may be covered by Medicaid in the 30 states that cover the medically indigent, if they meet the financial and categorical eligibility criteria.

INSURANCE COVERAGE AND
REGULAR SOURCE OF CARE

The literature cited in Chapters 1 and 2 suggests that low-income children are more likely than higher-income children to report a particular place as a regular source of care whereas higher-income children tend to have a physician's office as a regular source. This disparity has been attributed, in part, to the effects of Medicaid. However, data have not been published on the regular source of care of low-income children, according to their insurance coverage. This section presents such data, as well as information on the "convenience" of the regular source, measured by the average travel and waiting times. These data reflect indicators of "potential" access, as discussed in Chapter 1.

Overall, 85 percent of the low-income children were reported to have a regular source of care, ranging from 82 percent for those who were uninsured to 87 percent for the privately insured. (See Table 7.) Children covered by Medicaid part of the year were most likely to report a physician's office as a regular source (59 percent), probably due to their lower health status and thus, greater need for specialized care. Uninsured children were least likely to report a physician's office as a regular source (49 percent). In addition, non-Medicaid children were most likely to report a particular place as a regular source of care. These differences, however, were not statistically significant.

Of those with a regular source of care, the average travel time was 18 minutes, while the average waiting time in the physician's office, health center, or other place was 43 minutes. (See Table 8.) Average travel time was lower (although not significantly lower) for the privately insured children (16.3 minutes), compared to the uninsured (20.8 minutes), the part year Medicaid children (19.2 minutes), and the full year Medicaid children (18.6 minutes). Compared to the privately insured children, only the children on Medicaid the full year had a significantly longer waiting time (on average). Thus, it would appear from these data that there are few significant differences among Medicaid and non-Medicaid low-income children in the type of regular source and its convenience.

HEALTH SERVICE USE AND
INSURANCE COVERAGE

This section provides descriptive data on health service utilization by low-income children, according to type of insurance coverage. The data are presented unadjusted, and then adjusted for selected factors (self-reported health status, whether the child had a regular source of care, and age.)

Low-income children had significantly fewer physician visits than nonpoor children, 2.7 versus 3.3 visits per child. However, the number of visits per child with at least one visit was not significantly different, 3.8 visits for low-income children and 4.2 visits for nonpoor children. (See Table 9.)

Within the low-income population, non-Medicaid children were significantly less likely than Medicaid children to have a physician visit--33 percent of the non-Medicaid children had no physician visits in 1980. Uninsured children had an average of 1.8 physician visits, significantly less than the averages for the other three groups. In fact, the average number of visits for children covered by Medicaid part of the year was twice the level for uninsured children.

TABLE 7

REGULAR SOURCE OF CARE AND INSURANCE COVERAGE:
LOW-INCOME CHILDREN, UNITED STATES, 1980

| | | WITH REGULAR SOURCE | | |
| | | Physician's | Particular | No Regular |
Type of Coverage	Total	Office	Place	Source
Total	100.0	52.3	32.6	15.1
Medicaid coverage in 1980	100.0	53.6	30.6	15.8
Full year	100.0	52.5	32.2	15.3
Part year	100.0	58.5	23.6	17.9
No Medicaid coverage in 1980	100.0	51.1	34.3	14.6
Privately insured	100.0	52.2	34.8	13.0
Uninsured	100.0	48.6	33.2	18.2

Source: 1980 National Medical Care Utilization and Expenditure Survey.

TABLE 8

CONVENIENCE OF REGULAR SOURCE OF CARE FOR THOSE WITH A REGULAR SOURCE:
LOW-INCOME CHILDREN, UNITED STATES, 1980

| Type of Coverage | TYPE OF REGULAR SOURCE | | | CONVENIENCE OF REGULAR SOURCE | |
	Total	Physician's Office	Particular Place	Travel Time	Waiting Time
	Percent Distribution			Average Time (Minutes)	
Total	100.0	61.6	38.4	18.1	43.0
Medicaid coverage in 1980	100.0	63.7	36.3	18.7	46.8
Full year	100.0	61.9	38.1	18.6	48.9
Part year	100.0	71.3	28.7	19.2	37.8
No Medicaid coverage in 1980	100.0	59.8	40.2	17.5	39.8
Privately insured	100.0	60.0	40.0	16.3	35.4
Uninsured	100.0	59.4	40.6	20.8	51.1

Note: The population figures (in thousands) for this table are as follows: Total (14,295);
Medicaid full year (5,291); Medicaid part year (1,213); Privately
insured (5,588); and Uninsured (2,204).

Source: 1980 National Medical Care Utilization and Expenditure Survey.

TABLE 9

PHYSICIAN VISITS, ACCORDING TO INSURANCE COVERAGE:
LOW–INCOME CHILDREN, UNITED STATES, 1980

NUMBER OF PHYSICIAN VISITS

Type of Coverage	Total	No Visits	1 or 2 Visits	3 to 6 Visits	7 or more Visits	Visits per Child	Visits per Child With Visit
		Percent Distribution of Children				Average Number	
Total (all children)	100.0	23.6	37.5	26.7	12.3	3.1	4.1
Total (non-poor children)	100.0	21.6	38.1	27.5	12.7	3.3	4.2
Total (low–income)	100.0	29.0	35.6	24.3	11.1	2.7	3.8
Medicaid coverage in 1980	100.0	24.8	35.6	25.9	13.7	2.9	3.9
Full year	100.0	26.6	35.8	25.6	12.0	2.8	3.8
Part year	100.0	17.0	35.2	27.0	20.8	3.6	4.4
No Medicaid coverage in 1980	100.0	32.6	35.5	23.0	8.9	2.5	3.8
Privately insured	100.0	31.0	33.8	24.7	10.4	2.8	4.1
Uninsured	100.0	36.3	39.5	18.9	5.3 *	1.8	2.8

*Relative standard error equal to or greater than 0.30.

Source: 1980 National Medical Care Utilization and Expenditure Survey.

Another comparative measure is the average number of visits per child with at least one visit. Because this measure excludes children with no visits, it reflects the intensity of physician contact among users. The average number of visits per child with at least one visit ranged from 2.8 visits (uninsured) to 4.4 (part year Medicaid). Again, the uninsured had significantly fewer visits than each of the other three groups.

Although Table 9 clearly indicates that uninsured children were less likely than insured children to see a physician, it is inappropriate to make such a comparison without adjusting for perceived health status. Using the direct method of adjustment, disparities remained between insured and uninsured children in the percent with no physician visits in 1980; uninsured, 36.3 percent; privately insured, 30.6 percent; Medicaid full year, 26.9 percent; and Medicaid part year, 17.1 percent.

Another comparison was made adjusting for whether the child had a regular source of care. (See Table 10.) Having a regular source did not increase the likelihood of a physician visit among uninsured children; nor was it reduced. Slightly more than one-third of the uninsured children had no physician visits in 1980, regardless of whether they had a regular source of care. In contrast, for the children on Medicaid all year and the privately insured, the likelihood of a physician visit was significantly higher among children with a regular source. (The estimates for the part-year Medicaid children are unreliable due to the small sample size.)

The average number of visits for children with a regular source generally was not significantly different from the average for the children with no regular source with one exception. Privately insured children with a regular source averaged twice as many visits as those with no regular source (3.0 versus 1.6).

About one-half of the low-income children had no visits to an office-based physician in 1980. (See Table 11.) The average number of visits to a private physician was 1.3 visits. Of those with at least one visit, the average number per child was 2.7 visits. Children on Medicaid part of the year were most likely to visit private physicians although the differences among the four groups were not statistically significant.

Children on Medicaid part of the year had an average of 1.9 visits to a private physician, but among those making at least one visit, the average was 3.6 visits. The average number of visits for this group was significantly higher than the average for the other three groups. These figures, as well as the data presented above on aggregate physician use, are consistent with the notion that the children on Medicaid part-year are "medically needy."

Overall, 18 percent of the low-income children had one or more preventive visits in 1980. Because of varying protocols for preventive care depending on the age of the child, the data in Table 12 are shown by age. Children under age 6 were twice as likely (26 percent) as school-age children

TABLE 10

PHYSICIAN VISITS, ACCORDING TO REGULAR SOURCE OF CARE AND
INSURANCE COVERAGE: LOW–INCOME CHILDREN, UNITED STATES, 1980

Type of Coverage	CHILDREN WITH ONE OR MORE VISITS		VISITS PER CHILD	
	Regular Source	No Regular Source	Regular Source	No Regular Source
	Percent of Children		Average Number	
Total	72.7	61.4	2.9	1.8
Medicaid coverage in 1980	76.7	67.3	3.1	2.1
Full year	75.7	60.7	2.9	1.9
Part year	81.1	91.3	3.8	2.6 *
No Medicaid coverage in 1980	69.3	56.0	2.7	1.5
Privately insured	71.5	51.9	3.0	1.6
Uninsured	63.8	63.0	1.9	1.5

*Relative standard error equal to or greater than 0.30.

Source: 1980 National Medical Care Utilization and Expenditure Survey.

TABLE 11

VISITS TO PRIVATE PHYSICIANS, ACCORDING TO INSURANCE COVERAGE: LOW-INCOME CHILDREN, UNITED STATES, 1980

NUMBER OF PRIVATE PHYSICIAN VISITS

Type of Coverage	Total	No Visits	1 or 2 Visits	3 to 6 Visits	7 or more Visits	Visits per Child	Visits per Child With Visit
		Percent Distribution of Children				Average Number	
Total	100.0	52.2	30.9	13.2	3.8	1.3	2.7
Medicaid coverage in 1980	100.0	49.2	31.3	14.4	5.2	1.4	2.8
Full year	100.0	50.2	32.1	13.4	4.4	1.3	2.7
Part year	100.0	45.1	27.7	18.7	8.6	1.9	2.7
No Medicaid coverage in 1980	100.0	54.7	30.6	12.2	2.5	1.2	2.6
Privately insured	100.0	55.5	29.9	11.5	3.2	1.2	2.7
Uninsured	100.0	52.9	32.9	13.8	1.0*	1.1	2.3

*Relative standard error equal to or greater than 0.30.

Source: 1980 National Medical Care Utilization and Expenditure Survey.

TABLE 12

PREVENTIVE VISITS, ACCORDING TO CHILD'S AGE AND
INSURANCE COVERAGE: LOW-INCOME CHILDREN, UNITED STATES, 1980

Type of Coverage	Number of Children (in 000s)	All Ages	Under Age 6	Ages 6–11	Ages 12–17	Age-adjusted*
			Percent of Children			
Total	16,846	17.5	26.4	11.4	13.1	17.5
Medicaid coverage in 1980	7,725	21.7	30.8	14.8	16.5	21.2
Full year	6,248	21.5	31.9	14.0	15.1	21.0
Part year	1,478	22.4	26.1	19.3	20.5	22.2
No Medicaid coverage in 1980	9,120	13.9	22.0	8.8	10.5	14.6
Privately insured	6,425	14.3	21.9	9.6	11.0	14.2
Uninsured	2,695	12.9	22.2	7.0	8.9	13.2

*Age-adjusted by the direct method.

Source: 1980 National Medical Care Utilization and Expenditure Survey.

(11 percent) and adolescents (13 percent) to have a preventive exam. In all age groups, children covered by Medicaid were more likely to receive preventive care than children who were not covered by Medicaid, although the difference is significant only among the youngest children. This pattern is also observed when the figures are age-adjusted. Within the youngest age group, children on Medicaid the entire year were more likely to have a preventive exam than privately insured children. However, the probabilities for the part year Medicaid children and the uninsured children were not significantly different from the full year Medicaid children.

These comparisons provide descriptive data only, and further adjustments using more sophisticated statistical techniques will be made in Chapter 5.

PLACE OF VISIT AND INSURANCE COVERAGE

Differences in the place of visit according to type of insurance coverage may be an indicator of the nature of supply-side incentives as well as a reflection of individual preferences. For example, low-levels of physician reimbursement under Medicaid may reduce the availability of office-based care for Medicaid recipients and increase the use of hospital-based ambulatory care from outpatient departments (OPDs) and emergency rooms (ERs). Similarly, limited coverage of physicians' services among those who are privately insured may also lead to the use of hospital-based care. Additionally, utilization patterns may reflect an individual's or a group's preferences for office-based or hospital-based ambulatory care (subject to supply constraints).

Table 13 (top panel) shows the percent of children with at least one physician visit, who had visits to the specified places. Of the low-income children with a physician visit in 1980, 68 percent visited a physician's office, 29 percent went to a health center, 35 percent to an ER, and 25 percent to a hospital OPD. Compared to nonpoor children, the low-income children were significantly less likely to visit a physician's office, and more likely to use each of the three other facilities. (There were no significant differences in the percent of visits to "other" places, including laboratory and home visits, and visits to unspecified places.)

Within the low-income population, utilization patterns varied according to a child's insurance coverage. About 45 percent of the children on Medicaid part of the year (who used any ambulatory care), had one or more visits to an emergency room. In addition, children on Medicaid full year or part year (and who had at least one visit) were more likely than non-Medicaid children to visit a health center/clinic, perhaps because of the effort among community health centers to serve Medicaid recipients. There were no

TABLE 13

PHYSICIAN VISITS, ACCORDING TO PLACE OF VISIT AND INSURANCE COVERAGE

			PLACE OF VISIT**			
Type of Coverage	Total* (in 000s)	Physician's Office	Health Center or Clinic	ER	OPD	Other
		Percent of Children With at Least One Visit***				
Total (all children)	48,821	79.8	19.5	29.2	16.3	9.7
Total (nonpoor children)	36,865	83.7	16.5	27.2	13.5	9.6
Total (low-income children)	11,956	67.8	28.7	35.2	24.8	10.1
Medicaid coverage in 1980	5,810	67.5	34.1	36.9	24.1	10.2
Full year	4,585	68.1	33.6	34.9	24.7	10.2
Part year	1,226	65.3	35.6	44.5	21.5	10.4
No Medicaid coverage in 1980	6,146	68.0	23.7	33.6	25.5	9.9
Privately insured	4,430	66.1	23.0	35.6	27.2	10.8
Uninsured	1,716	73.0	25.5	28.5	21.3	7.7
		Percent of Visits				
Total (all children)	199,911	66.8	9.3	10.0	10.4	3.5
Total (nonpoor children)	154,120	71.9	8.4	8.7	7.3	3.6
Total (low-income children)	45,792	49.5	12.2	14.3	20.8	3.2
Medicaid coverage in 1980	22,649	50.4	15.1	15.9	15.3	3.2
Full year	17,288	49.3	16.2	15.6	15.6	3.3
Part year	5,361	54.0	11.4	16.9	14.7	3.0
No Medicaid coverage in 1980	23,142	48.6	9.5	12.7	26.1	3.2
Privately insured	18,255	45.5	9.1	12.5	29.4	3.2
Uninsured	4,887	59.0	10.7	13.5	13.7	3.1

*The totals in the top panel are the number of children (in thousands) with at least one visit. The totals in the bottom panel are the number of visits (in thousands).

**Excludes telephone contacts. Health center/clinic includes visits to community health centers, school clinics, etc. Other includes laboratory and home visits as well as visits to unspecified places.

***Some children visited more than one place. Therefore, the rows do not sum to 100 percent.

Source: 1980 National Medical Care Utilization and Expenditure Survey.

statistical differences in the use of OPDs, office-based physicians, and other places among the four groups.

Table 13 (bottom panel) shows the percent distribution of visits, according to place of visit. Among nonpoor children, visits to a physician's office accounted for over two-thirds of the visits, compared to one-half for the low-income children. A higher proportion of the visits among low-income children were to organized settings (health centers/clinics, hospital emergency rooms, outpatient departments). In particular, the percent of visits by low-income children to hospital OPDs was about three times that by nonpoor children.

Within the low-income population, uninsured children had the highest percent of visits to a physician's office, while privately insured children had the lowest (although this difference was not significant). Unexpectedly, the privately insured children had the highest percentage of visits to hospital outpatient departments (although this difference, also, was not significant at the 0.05 level).[2] Compared to non-Medicaid children, the Medicaid children (full and part year combined) did have a significantly higher percent of visits to health centers as well as to hospital emergency rooms.

Two points should be emphasized about Table 13. Clearly, low-income children who have any ambulatory care make greater use of hospital-based facilities compared to children of all incomes. However, within the low-income population, a higher proportion of the privately insured children used such facilities.

The higher use of hospital OPDs and ERs has both "cost" and "quality" implications. The average charge for a hospital ER visit in 1980 was $77.21, compared to $44.86 for an OPD visit, $22.09 for an office visit, and $21.06 for a clinic visit. (These data are from the 1980 NMCUES based on visits by low-income children that had a charge.) Clearly, visits to a physician's office or to a health center are lower in cost than those to an OPD or ER. Thus, from a cost perspective, OPDs and ERs should be providers of last resort.

From a quality perspective, ERs in particular are generally considered inappropriate providers of primary care or nonurgent care, because they lack continuity and comprehensiveness. As Davidson (1978) notes: "Nonurgent care provided in ERs necessarily lacks continuity and followup, for one thing, since ERs must be established to respond to emergency episodes. Furthermore, ER personnel are trained and selected for their ability to treat emergency and urgent conditions: in many instances they have neither the experience nor the interest needed to provide effective primary care."

EXPENDITURES FOR PHYSICIANS' SERVICES
ACCORDING TO INSURANCE COVERAGE

In 1980, $1.4 billion reportedly was spent for physician visits by low-income children. Expenditures for physicians' services are a function of two components: the number of visits and the cost per visit. An additional factor affects the estimates that are obtained from a household survey such as the NMCUES, that is, the individual's knowledge of the "cost" of care. The expenditure data are based on reported charges, not the actual cost of care. Thus, the data underestimate the amounts for subsidized care (e.g., community health centers and public hospitals).

The reported charges were disproportionately high (relative to the distribution of children) for children covered by Medicaid part-year and those who were privately insured. In contrast, they were disproportionately low for uninsured children. (See Table 14.) The differentials in charges are also illustrated by the average charge per child and the average charge per visit, as shown in Table 15. (These estimates are based on children/visits with charges, and exclude those with no charges.) Children on Medicaid full year or part year and those who were privately insured had significantly higher average charges than the uninsured children.

The considerably lower charges among uninsured children deserves further comment. While the previous analysis indicated that the uninsured had fewer visits than other children, it was not on the order of magnitude that the lower average charges per child would suggest. Clearly, subsidized care accounts for a large amount of this difference. The average charge per visit for uninsured children was less than that for the three other groups, for office visits as well as visits to ERs and OPDs (data not shown).

Finally, the level of out-of-pocket expenditures, according to insurance coverage, is as one would expect: the uninsured and the privately insured bear a significantly higher burden than the Medicaid children (See Table 16.) The average expense for non-Medicaid children ($42.27) was more than triple the average expense for Medicaid children ($13.47). However, the children on Medicaid part of the year had significantly higher out-of-pocket expense than those covered by Medicaid the full year ($26.51 versus $9.98). In part, this may be due to the "spend-down" requirements to qualify for a states' medically needy program under Medicaid.

It should be noted that these data on out-of-pocket expenditures related only to physician visits. Expenditures for inpatient hospital care, dental care, and prescribed medicines, are not shown in Table 16. Those data show that 13 percent of the low-income children had $100 or more in such expenses for all types of medical care (including 3 percent of the full year Medicaid children; 17 percent of the part year Medicaid children; 21 percent of the privately insured; and 17 percent of the uninsured.)

TABLE 14

EXPENDITURES FOR PHYSICIANS' SERVICES, ACCORDING TO
INSURANCE COVERAGE: LOW-INCOME CHILDREN,
UNITED STATES, 1980

Type of Coverage	Number of Children (in 000s)	Percent of Children	Total Expenditures* (in 000s)	Percent of Expenditures
Total	16,846	100.0	$ 1,427,057	100.0
Medicaid coverage in 1980	7,725	45.9	692,089	48.5
Full year	6,248	37.1	514,598	36.1
Part year	1,478	8.8	177,491	12.4
No Medicaid coverage in 1980	9,120	54.1	734,969	51.5
Privately insured	6,425	38.1	632,839	44.3
Uninsured	2,695	16.0	102,130	7.2

*The figures in this column represent the expenditures for children in
each of the insurance categories. They do not represent the amounts
spent by Medicaid for those covered full or part year, nor by private
insurers for those who were privately insured. (Payments for insurance
premiums also are excluded.) These figures are the sum of all sources of
payment on behalf of children in each of the groups.

Source: 1980 National Medical Care Utilization and Expenditure Survey.

TABLE 15

AVERAGE CHARGE PER CHILD AND PER PHYSICIAN VISIT, ACCORDING TO INSURANCE COVERAGE: LOW-INCOME CHILDREN, UNITED STATES, 1980

| Type of Coverage | NUMBER OF CHILDREN | | | NUMBER OF VISITS | | |
	Total (in 000s)	With Visit	With Charge	Average Charge Per Child With Charge	Total (in 000s)	With Charge	Average Charge Per Visit With Charge
Total	16,846	11,956	11,347	$125.77	45,792	40,555	$35.19
Medicaid coverage in 1980	7,726	5,810	5,545	$124.82	22,649	19,780	$34.99
Full year	6,248	4,585	4,366	$117.85	17,288	15,037	$34.22
Part year	1,478	1,226	1,178	$150.64	5,361	4,743	$37.42
No Medicaid coverage in 1980	9,120	6,146	5,802	$126.67	23,142	20,775	$35.38
Privately insured	6,425	4,430	4,216	$150.09	18,255	16,454	$38.46
Uninsured	2,695	1,716	1,586	$64.40	4,887	4,320	$23.64

Note: The average charges per child and per visit include charges that were imputed. Altogether 58 percent of the charges were imputed, ranging from 21 percent for those who were uninsured, to 86 percent for those who had Medicaid only the entire year.

Source: 1980 National Medical Care Utilization and Expenditure Survey.

TABLE 16

OUT-OF-POCKET (OOP) EXPENDITURES FOR PHYSICIAN VISITS, ACCORDING TO INSURANCE COVERAGE: LOW-INCOME CHILDREN, UNITED STATES, 1980

Type of Coverage	Total	None	$1–49	$50–99	$100 or More	No Contact	Average OOP Expenditures*
				Percent Distribution of Children			
Total	100.0	36.3	21.2	8.2	5.2	29.0	$28.27
Medicaid coverage in 1980	100.0	58.6	10.7	4.0	2.0	24.8	$13.47
Full year	100.0	62.5	7.5	2.2	1.2 **	26.6	$9.98
Part year	100.0	41.9	24.4	11.8	5.0 **	17.0	$26.51
No Medicaid coverage in 1980	100.0	17.5	30.1	11.7	8.0	32.6	$42.27
Privately insured	100.0	19.8	30.9	10.4	7.8	31.0	$39.22
Uninsured	100.0	12.1	28.4	14.7	8.5	36.3	$50.16

*Average based only on children with one or more physician visits.

**Relative standard error equal to or greater than 0.30.

Source: 1980 National Medical Care Utilization and Expenditure Survey.

NOTES

1. The NMCUES estimate of the poverty population is reasonably comparable to data from the Current Population Survey (CPS). According to the NMCUES, there were 9.8 million children under age 18 living below the poverty level in 1980. The figure from the 1981 CPS was 11.1 million related children under age 18 (U.S. Bureau of the Census, 1982). This represents a difference of 1.3 million children or 13.3 percent. This difference may result from three factors. First, the NMCUES estimate excludes children who were born, or died, or who were institutionalized in 1980, as well as others who were not eligible to participate in the survey for the entire year. Only institutionalized children were excluded from the CPS estimate. Second, income may be more accurately reported in the NMCUES because the data collection consisted of four or five interviews, roughly every three months. In contrast, the March 1981 CPS asked for recall of all income for 1980. Data on non-wage income, in particular, may be more complete in the NMCUES. Finally, the NMCUES employs slightly different poverty thresholds that do not distinguish between farm and non-farm families and that do not take into account the number of children in the family. The net effect of these three factors is to lower the NMCUES estimate of the number of children in poverty.

2. The differences in the percent of visits to OPDs were not statistically significant at the 0.05 level, due to a high relative standard error (RSE) of the estimate for the privately insured children (RSE = 26.0). These differences are significant at the 0.10 level.

Chapter 5

DETERMINANTS OF PHYSICIAN
USE BY LOW-INCOME CHILDREN:
EMPIRICAL FINDINGS

As discussed in Chapter 4, some of the utilization patterns among low-income children covered by Medicaid differs from those not on Medicaid. This chapter employs multiple regression analysis to statistically control for the various factors that are expected to influence physician use, and to evaluate the independent effect of each factor on physician use.

The first section of this chapter analyzes the relative effect of Medicaid coverage on various types of utilization, controlling for sociodemographic characteristics, economic factors, organizational variables, community resources, and health status measures. The second section focuses on children with a regular source of care, to determine the importance of "time costs," that is, travel and waiting times, relative to other factors. Finally, the determinants of physician use for Medicaid and non-Medicaid children are evaluated separately and compared. The discussion of the results is organized according to the five groups of independent variables specified in Chapter 3 (Table 2) and displayed in Figure 3.

EFFECTS OF INDEPENDENT VARIABLES

Maximum likelihood dichotomous logit equations for the dependent variables VSTALLMH, VSTPRVMH, PREVALL, and PREVPRIV are given in Table 17. Weighted least squares multiple regression equations for LOGALLMH and LOGPRVMH are given in Table 18. The findings for the economic factors are presented first.

FIGURE 3
MODEL OF HEALTH SERVICE USE BY LOW-INCOME CHILDREN

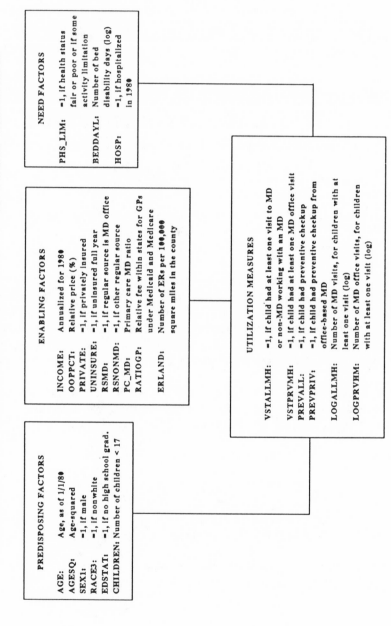

PREDISPOSING FACTORS

AGE: Age, as of 1/1/80
AGESQ: Age-squared
SEX1:   =1, if male
RACE3:   =1, if nonwhite
EDSTAT: =1, if no high school grad.
CHILDREN: Number of children < 17

ENABLING FACTORS

INCOME: Annualized for 1980
OOPPCT: Relative price (%)
PRIVATE: =1, if privately insured
UNINSURE: =1, if uninsured full year
RSMD: =1, if regular source is MD office
RSNONMD: =1, if other regular source
PC_MD: Primary care MD ratio
RATIOGP: Relative fee within states for GPs
          under Medicaid and Medicare
ERLAND: Number of ERs per 100,000
          square miles in the county

NEED FACTORS

PHS_LIM: =1, if health status
          fair or poor or if some
          activity limitation
BEDDAYL: Number of bed
          disability days (log)
HOSP: =1, if hospitalized
          in 1980

UTILIZATION MEASURES

VSTALLMH: =1, if child had at least one visit to MD
          or non-MD working with an MD
VSTPRVMH: =1, if child had at least one MD office visit
PREVALL: =1, if child had preventive checkup
PREVPRIV: =1, if child had preventive checkup from
          office-based MD
LOGALLMH: Number of MD visits, for children with at
          least one visit (log)
LOGPRVHM: Number of MD office visits, for children
          with at least one visit (log)

TABLE 17

MAXIMUM LIKELIHOOD DICHOTOMOUS LOGIT EQUATIONS:
ALL LOW–INCOME CHILDREN (t–values in parentheses)

Variable	VSTALLMH (Eq. 1)	VSTPRVMH (Eq. 2)	PREVALL (Eq. 3)	PREVPRIV (Eq. 4)
REALAGE	−0.235 (3.94)	−0.132 (2.69)	−0.213 (4.06)	−0.354 (4.75)
AGESQ	0.010 (2.88)	0.007 (2.37)	0.009 (2.94)	0.018 (4.18)
SEX1	--	--	--	−0.335 (1.46)
RACE3	−0.173 (0.82)	−0.329 (1.98)	−0.081 (0.35)	−0.521 (1.61)
EDSTAT	−0.229 (1.43)	−0.203 (1.24)	−0.175 (0.82)	−0.257 (0.82)
CHILDREN	−0.177 (3.03)	−0.233 (4.80)	−0.183 (3.14)	−0.317 (3.59)
INCOME	−6.7E−5 (2.67)	−1.5E−5 (0.72)	−4.1E−5 (1.62)	−1.8E−5 (0.55)
PRIVATE	−0.368 (1.81)	−0.610 (3.01)	−0.349 (1.66)	−0.531 (1.73)
UNINSURE	−0.562 (1.90)	−0.502 (2.01)	−0.438 (1.57)	−0.016 (0.03)
PC_MD	−3.0E−4 (1.14)	−6.0E−4 (2.84)	−3.1E−5 (0.10)	−1.0E−4 (0.30)
RATIOGP	0.105 (0.28)	0.565 (1.40)	−0.873 (1.94)	−0.096 (0.14)

TABLE 17 (continued)

MAXIMUM LIKELIHOOD DICHOTOMOUS LOGIT EQUATIONS:
ALL LOW–INCOME CHILDREN (t–values in parentheses)

ERLAND	1.450	–6.4E–5	2.5E–4	–7.4E–4
	(3.62)	(0.17)	(0.81)	(1.31)
PHS_LIM	0.629	0.498	0.232	0.140
	(2.10)	(2.38)	(0.79)	(0.41)
BEDDAYL	0.595	0.459	0.084	–0.065
	(5.41)	(5.79)	(0.94)	(0.59)
HOSP	1.205	0.431	0.061	0.075
	(1.90)	(1.46)	(0.18)	(0.21)
CONSTANT	2.699	0.733	0.973	0.597
	(6.14)	(1.83)	(1.91)	(0.82)
ADJUSTED R–SQ (SRS)	0.267	0.090	0.050	0.073
R–SQ (CSD)	0.034	0.019	0.006	0.006
n	1,363	1,363	1,363	1,363
CHI–SQ	464.30	197.56	92.06	89.08

Notes:
1. The t–values were calculated after adjustments for the
   complex sample design. The critical t–ratio at the
   5 percent level of significance is 1.96 for a two–tailed test.

2. R–SQ (SRS) refers to the proportion of variance explained
   under simple random sampling assumptions. R–SQ (CSD) refers
   to the proportion of variance explained when the complex sample
   design is taken into account. The second value is much lower
   because of the restrictions on the degrees of freedom based on
   the number of PSUs.

3. E(integer) signifies that the value should be multiplied by the
   indicated power of ten.

Source: 1980 National Medical Care Utilization and Expenditure Survey.

TABLE 18

WEIGHTED LEAST SQUARES REGRESSION EQUATIONS:
ALL LOW–INCOME CHILDREN (t–values in parentheses)

Variable	LOGALLMH (Eq. 5)	LOGALLMH (Eq. 6)	LOGPRVMH (Eq. 7)	LOGPRVMH (Eq. 8)
REALAGE	-0.115	-0.112	-0.102	-0.101
	(7.51)	(7.20)	(5.78)	(5.58)
AGESQ	0.006	0.006	0.006	0.006
	(6.40)	(5.99)	(5.80)	(5.62)
RACE3	-0.069	-0.075	-0.062	-0.072
	(1.10)	(1.25)	(0.90)	(1.08)
EDSTAT	-0.169	-0.150	-0.116	-0.119
	(3.37)	(3.10)	(2.08)	(2.09)
CHILDREN	-0.051	-0.046	-0.043	-0.037
	(3.62)	(2.93)	(2.49)	(2.19)
INCOME	-1.8E-5	-2.1E-5	2.8E-6	1.8E-6
	(2.64)	(2.75)	(0.32)	(0.20)
INCOME	-0.014	--	-0.012	--
	(4.47)		(3.30)	
PRIVATE	--	-0.016	--	-0.094
		(0.25)		(1.54)
UNINSURE	--	-0.168	--	-0.122
		(2.67)		(1.73)
RSMD	0.012	0.120	0.078	0.067
	(1.55)	(1.24)	(0.75)	(0.62)
RENONME	0.153	0.160	-0.215	-0.204
	(1.52)	(1.54)	(2.01)	(1.88)
PC_MD	-1.4E-4	-1.4E-4	-8.6E-5	-8.4E-5
	(1.71)	(1.74)	(1.25)	(1.29)
RATIOGP	-0.045	-0.066	-0.052	-0.060
	(0.32)	(0.46)	(0.37)	(0.44)

TABLE 18 (continued)

WEIGHTED LEAST SQUARES REGRESSION EQUATIONS:
ALL LOW-INCOME CHILDREN (t-values in parentheses)

ERLAND	2.8E-4	-2.9E-4	-9.5E-5	-8.5E-5
	(2.79)	(2.80)	(1.16)	(1.01)
PHS_LIM	0.401	0.413	0.257	0.265
	(5.47)	(5.68)	(3.26)	(3.38)
BEDDAYL	0.218	0.216	0.160	0.160
	(9.97)	(9.74)	(5.14)	(5.10)
HOSP	0.400	0.393	0.365	0.364
	(4.14)	(4.02)	(2.88)	(2.86)
CONSTANT	1.359	1.362	0.978	0.977
ADJUSTED R-SQ (SRS)	0.302	0.296	0.224	0.217
R-SQ (LSD)	0.097	0.093	0.056	0.054
n	972	972	639	639
CHI-SQ	63.53	51.20	16.58	16.06

Notes:

1. The t-values were calculated after adjustments for the complex sample design. The critical t-ratio at the 5 percent level of significance is 1.96 for a two-tailed test.

2. R-SQ (SRS) refers to the proportion of variance explained under simple random sampling assumptions. R-SQ (CSD) refers to the proportion of variance explained when the complex sample design is taken into account. The second value is much lower because of the restrictions on the degrees of freedom based on the number of PSUs.

3. E(integer) signifies that the value should be multiplied by the indicated power of ten.

Source: 1980 National Medical Care Utilization and Expenditure Survey.

TABLE 19

INCOME AND PRICE ELASTICITIES, ACCORDING TO INSURANCE
COVERAGE: LOW-INCOME CHILDREN, UNITED STATES, 1980

	LOGALLMH		LOGPRVMH	
	Mean	Elasticity	Mean	Elasticity
A. INCOME ELASTICITIES				
All low-income children	$8,113	-0.147	$8,421	0.034
Medicaid children	6,972	-0.128	7,014	0.028
Non-Medicaid children	9,365	-0.172	9,916	0.040
B. PRICE ELASTICITIES				
All low-income children	3.76	-0.055	4.66	-0.081
Low-income children with some out-of-pocket charge	7.87	-0.211	7.99	-0.228
Medicaid children	1.24	-0.018	1.38	-0.024
Non-Medicaid children	6.42	-0.094	8.15	-0.143

Note: Elasticities were calculated based on the income and price
         coefficients from the total sample (Table 18, Eq. 5 and 7) and the
         weighted means for the total sample and each of the subgroups.

Source: 1980 National Medical Care Utilization and Expenditure Survey.

Economic Factors

Income was not a significant factor in the use of private physicians' services or preventive care, but it was significantly and negatively related to the probability of any use (VSTALLMH), as well as the volume of visits among those with at least one visit (LOGALLMH). The negative income effect was not expected. Nevertheless it is likely that such an effect reflects the opportunity cost of a physician visit. Consider, for example, that as income rises, the likelihood of welfare eligibility (and Medicaid coverage) decreases. Above a certain threshold therefore, the parent may be employed in an hourly-wage position, with minimal or no sick-leave benefits. Thus, although income increases, another constraint may be imposed. A "cost" of taking a child to a physician could be the loss of a half or full day's wages, or at worst, the fear of losing one's job.

While the "opportunity cost" explanation of the negative income effect is plausible, there may be other explanations. For example, the income variable may be measuring the relationship between income and insurance coverage (i.e., poor children tend to have more comprehensive coverage under Medicaid than near-poor children who are privately insured or uninsured). Thus, a negative income coefficient may indirectly reflect the effect of Medicaid coverage. It should be noted, however, that the negative income effect applies to low-income children and not the population as a whole. In general, physicians' services are a positive good, such that increased income results in higher use. This finding should be explored using other data sets.

The income elasticity for the total sample (evaluated at the means) was -0.147 for physician visits, given at least one visit (LOGALLMH). (See Table 19, panel A.) Separate income elasticity estimates for the Medicaid and non-Medicaid children reveal that those not on Medicaid have a higher responsiveness to changes in income. In absolute terms, the estimate for the total sample is comparable to Inman's (1976) estimate for the nonworking mother's sample. However, unlike the other estimates reviewed in Chapter 2, a negative income elasticity was obtained in this study. Again, it should be remembered that the findings from this study apply to the low-income population rather than children of all incomes. (The INCOME coefficient for LOGPRVMH was nonsignificant and the corresponding elasticity is trivial.)

Insurance coverage, or the lack of it, appears not to be an important determinant of physician use in two equations.[1] Privately insured children (PRIVATE) and uninsured children (UNINSURE) had a lower probability of visiting a private physician (VSTPRVMH) than Medicaid children (the omitted category). With respect to the volume of visits among those with at least one visit (Table 18, eq. 6 and eq. 8), privately insured and uninsured children were not significantly different from Medicaid children in the number of visits to private physicians (LOGPRVMH), but uninsured children did have fewer visits overall (LOGALLMH).[2]

These results are important. They differ from those obtained from Colle and Grossman (1978) in their study of children of all incomes ages 1 to 5. They found that Medicaid increased the probability of any use as well as of preventive care, but the use of private physicians was lower. Within the low-income population (under age 18) this was not the case. The Medicaid children experienced a higher likelihood of seeing a private physician than privately insured and uninsured children; but among those who had at least one visit, there were no significant differences. For any type of visit, Medicaid coverage was not a significant factor in the *probability* of contact; however, Medicaid children who made one or more visits had more visits than uninsured children, other things being equal.

The "price" of a physician visit, measured as the percent of total charges paid out-of-pocket (OOPPCT) was significantly and negatively related to the volume of visits, both overall (LOGALLMH) and to a private physician (LOGPRVMH). That is, as the out-of-pocket charge increased, physician use decreased.

The price elasticity (evaluated at the means) for private physician visits was -0.081, compared to -0.055 for all visits. (See Table 19.) The higher price elasticity for visits to private physicians than for all visits suggests a possible quality-quantity substitution. As has been demonstrated elsewhere (Taube, 1984), the price elasticity is substantially higher when children with no out-of-pocket charges are excluded. The elasticities exceed -0.20 in both cases.

As shown in Table 19 (panel B), the price elasticity for Medicaid children was considerably less than that for non-Medicaid children. Of course, children on Medicaid have very low out-of-pocket charges so a low price elasticity would be expected. The non-Medicaid children had a price elasticity of -0.09 for all visits and -0.14 for private physician visits.

Table 20 displays the annual predicted utilization of Medicaid and non-Medicaid children, according to health status.[3] In all cases, the probability or volume of use was higher among Medicaid children than non-Medicaid children. However not all the differences were statistically significant. As discussed previously, Medicaid coverage significantly increased the likelihood of seeing a private physician. In addition, those with Medicaid coverage had more visits than uninsured children but not compared to privately insured children. Health status was a significant factor in the probability and volume of use for all measures except preventive care use.

This table shows that the probability of a physician visit for uninsured children in fair or poor health was lower than the probability for Medicaid children in excellent or good health, all other things being equal. Similarly,

TABLE 20

PREDICTED ANNUAL USE OF PHYSICIANS' SERVICES, ACCORDING TO INSURANCE COVERAGE: LOW-INCOME CHILDREN, UNITED STATES, 1980

Type of Use	CHILDREN IN EXCELLENT/GOOD HEALTH AND NO ACTIVITY LIMITATION			CHILDREN IN FAIR/POOR HEALTH OR WITH AN ACTIVITY LIMITATION		
	Medicaid	Privately Insured	Uninsured	Medicaid	Privately Insured	Uninsured
Probability of any visit	0.74	0.70	0.64	0.81	0.77	0.71
Probability of private physician visit	0.53	0.40 *	0.42 *	0.64	0.51 *	0.54 *
Probability of preventive visit	0.21	0.15	0.14	0.23	0.17	0.16
Probability of preventive visit to private physician	0.13	0.08	0.12	0.13	0.08	0.12
Number of physician visits**	2.64	2.60	2.23 *	3.98	3.92	3.37 *
Number of private physician visits***	2.05	1.86	1.81	2.67	2.43	2.36

*Probability or volume of use was significantly different (p<0.05) from Medicaid children.

**For those with at least one physician visit.

***For those with at least one visit to a private physician.

Note: The predicted utilization figures were derived by multiplying the coefficients from the regression equations by the mean values for the total sample, adjusting the assumptions about health status and insurance coverage.

Source: 1980 National Medical Care Utilization and Expenditure Survey.

privately insured children in fair or poor health were less likely to see a private physician than Medicaid children in excellent or good health.

Sociodemographic Characteristics

Physician use by low-income children has a U-shaped age effect, as demonstrated by the combined effect of REALAGE and AGESQ. This relationship was found for all six dependent variables. Controlling for other factors, the predicted number of visits among those with at least one visit (LOGALLMH) was highest for children ages 1 and 2 and lowest for those between ages 9 through 11. The predicted number of visits began rising at age 11, through age 17.[4]

Sex (SEX1) was not found to be a significant factor in the use of preventive care by private physicians (PREVPRIV). A higher likelihood among females was hypothesized, due to the use of fertility-related care during adolescence. (SEX1 was not significant in any of the other equations and was dropped in preliminary analyses because no difference was expected.)

Within the low-income population, white children had a higher likelihood than nonwhite children of a visit to a private physician (VSTPRVMH). Although the probability of contact with a private physician was lower among nonwhite children, those who had at least one visit to a private physician did not make fewer (or more) visits than white children (LOGPRVMH). There were no differences between white and nonwhite children in the probability or volume of use of other types of physicians' services (VSTALLMH, PREVALL, PREVPRIV, and LOGALLMH).

Children in families with at least one high school graduate did not have a higher probability of a physician visit, including preventive care. However, educational status was significantly related to the number of visits, with children in "more educated" families having a higher number of visits (LOGALLMH and LOGPRVMH).

These findings differ from Colle and Grossman's (1978) results about the effect of mother's schooling. They found that the probability of overall and preventive care use was higher, but the volume of visits was lower among children whose mothers had more schooling. In part, the difference may stem from the definition of educational status in the two studies. However, the difference may also be due to the scope of the samples: this study is limited to low-income children and includes children through age 17 (rather than limiting the sample to ages 1 to 5). Educational attainment, especially the mother's education, may substitute for health service use (in a production function context) within the preschool population and within a broader income range, as Colle and Grossman have shown. But when the age range is broader and the income range narrower, education may be a proxy for health beliefs and tastes rather than the household production of health.

The number of children in the family is negatively related to physician use for each of the six dependent variables. Various interpretations for this result have been offered in the literature: (1) the effect of many children on per capita income; (2) the indirect costs associated with seeing a physician, such as multiple public transportation fares, baby-sitter fees, or even the inconvenience of taking several children to a physician's office or other place; and (3) the substitution of parents' experience for physician use in caring for several children with the same or similar illnesses.

Organizational Variables

The effect of having a regular source has been a subject of much empirical research. Most studies reviewed in Chapter 2 found that the presence of a regular source was a significant factor in the use of medical care. In most study designs (including the present study), having a regular source is not independent of physician use. For this reason, the effect of the type of regular source was measured only in the volume equations (LOGALLMH and LOGPRVMH). The purpose was to assess the effect of a regular source on the volume of visits.

The presence of a regular source, either a physician's office (RSMD) or other place (RSNONMD), had little or no effect on the number of visits among those with at least one visit. The only significant result was obtained with respect to private physician visits (LOGPRVMH): as would be expected, a place other than a physician's office as a regular source (RSNONMD) was found to be negatively related to the number of private physician visits ($p = 0.049$). These findings provide some evidence that having a regular source of care is not associated with a higher level of use, among those who make at least one visit.

The next section of this chapter will examine the determinants of use among those with a regular source.

Community Resources

The availability of office-based primary care physicians (PC_MD) was significantly related to the probability of private physician visits (VSTPRVMH). Unexpectedly, the coefficient had a negative sign, meaning that children in counties with high physician-per-population ratios were less likely to visit a private physician. A possible interpretation is that physicians in counties with high rates of primary care physicians per population are competing for the higher-income patients (with broader private insurance coverage and higher rates of reimbursement), rather than serving the low-income patient with low levels of Medicaid reimbursement, narrow insurance coverage for ambulatory care, or no insurance coverage for ambulatory care, or no insurance coverage whatsoever. Alternatively, areas with a high ratio of office-based physicians per population also tend to have more non-office-based facilities, such as outpatient departments, community health centers, and public health clinics. A third explanation is that physicians may locate in areas of a county that are not low-income. Thus, it would be possible for counties to have a high rate of physicians-per-population but low rates in inner-city areas where the low-income are concentrated. This problem has been noted by the President's Commission for the Study of Ethical Problems in Medicine and Biomedical and Behavioral Research (1983).[5]

Neither of these interpretations was borne out in the regression analysis, where the level of Medicaid reimbursement (RATIOGP) and availability of emergency rooms (ERLAND) were not significantly related to the use of private physicians (VSTPRVMH and LOGPRVMH).[6]

An unexpected result is that the probability of a preventive visit (PREVALL) was inversely related (p=0.06) to the Medicaid reimbursement level (RATIOGP). A possible, although untested, explanation is that low-income children may receive preventive care from sources that are not sensitive to the level of Medicaid reimbursement (such as health centers, public health clinics, or school clinics).

The availability of hospital emergency rooms (ERLAND) was a significant factor in the probability and volume of use of physicians' services (VSTALLMH and LOGALLMH), but not in any other type of use. Thus, as the availability of emergency rooms increases, use increases. This suggests that emergency rooms are still an important source of care for low-income children despite efforts to develop alternate sources of care (including hospital-based primary care centers and community health centers).

Health Status Measures

As other studies have shown, health status measures were the single most important group of variables that determine who uses physicians' services and how much. These variables, however, were not significant determinants of the use of preventive care (and were not expected to be significant factors). Two of the three health status measures (PHS_LIM and BEDDAYL) were significant in the four equations concerning physician use: VSTALLMH, VSTPRVMH, LOGALLMH, and LOGPRVMH. In other words, the likelihood and volume of use was higher among those in fair or poor health status or with an activity limitation. Use was higher when the number of bed-days was higher. The direction of causality between bed-days and use is not clear because physician use may lead to bed-days, or bed-days may lead to physician use.

A hospitalization in 1980 was not a significant determinant of the likelihood of physician use (overall as well as the use of private physicians).

However, children that were hospitalized during 1980 had more visits than those who were not hospitalized (but who had at least one physician visit).

CHILDREN WITH A REGULAR SOURCE

This section examines the determinants of use among children with a regular source of care, focusing on three areas: the effect of travel and waiting time, the effect of Medicaid coverage, and the magnitude of price and income elasticities.

Effect of Travel and Waiting Time

Equations 9 through 16 (Tables 21 and 22) tested the effect of travel and waiting times on the use of physicians' services. In none of the equations was travel time (TRAVEL) significant at the 0.05 level. Waiting time (WAIT) was a significant factor in the likelihood of visiting a private physician (VSTPRVMH). As waiting time increased, the probability of making such a visit decreased.

In two equations, VSTPRVMH and PREVPRIV, the presence of a physician's office as a regular source (RSMD) was positively related to the probability of use. This finding, in itself, is not surprising because of the interrelationship between having a physician's office as a regular source and visiting a private physician. What is of interest is that those with a physician's office as a regular source had, on average, significantly less waiting time than those with another type of regular source--33 minutes versus 58 minutes. It may be, therefore, that the measure of type of regular source (RSMD) is reflecting a preference for a more "convenient" and less time-consuming source of care.

Effect of Medicaid Coverage

In this subsample, limited to children with a regular source of care, the only difference between Medicaid and non-Medicaid children was in the likelihood of using private physicians' services (VSTPRVMH). In the total sample, it may be recalled, both privately insured and uninsured children were significantly less likely to visit a private physician. However, among those with a regular source, only privately insured children had a lower probability of such use. Uninsured children with a regular source were no less likely than Medicaid children with a regular source to see a private physician.

As reported for the total sample, there were no differences between Medicaid and non-Medicaid children with a regular source in the number of visits to private physicians (LOGPRVMH). However, uninsured children with

TABLE 21

MAXIMUM LIKELIHOOD DICHOTOMOUS LOGIT EQUATIONS:
CHILDREN WITH A REGULAR SOURCE (t-values in parentheses)

Variable	VSTALLMH (Eq. 9)	VSTPRVMH (Eq. 10)	PREVALL (Eq. 11)	PREVPRIV (Eq. 12)
REALAGE	-0.223 (3.34)	-0.125 (2.42)	-0.220 (3.89)	-0.358 (3.80)
AGESQ	0.010 (2.44)	0.006 (2.15)	0.010 (2.92)	0.018 (1.52)
SEX1	--	--	--	-0.330 (1.52)
RACE3	-0.216 (0.94)	-0.183 (0.88)	-0.126 (0.51)	-0.384 (0.99)
EDSTAT	-0.251 (2.18)	-0.106 (0.59)	-0.119 (0.51)	-0.166 (0.47)
CHILDREN	-0.177 (2.93)	-0.229 (3.27)	-0.210 (3.21)	-0.313 (2.98)
INCOME	-6.3E-5 (2.30)	-1.1E-5 (0.51)	-4.0E-5 (1.55)	-3.5E-5 (1.11)
PRIVATE	-0.330 (1.60)	-0.465 (2.47)	-0.337 (1.59)	-0.354 (1.10)
UNINSURE	-0.548 (1.80)	-0.223 (0.83)	-0.374 (1.42)	0.175 (0.45)
RSMD	0.091 (0.44)	1.395 (7.59)	-0.110 (0.62)	1.152 (3.79)
TRAVEL	-0.002 (0.36)	0.009 (1.68)	-0.008 (1.18)	0.006 (0.72)
WAIT	-9.7E-4 (0.43)	-0.005 (2.85)	-0.001 (0.69)	-0.002 (0.58)
PC_MD	-2.8E-4 (0.98)	-3.2E-4 (1.34)	-4.4E-5 (0.13)	5.9E-5 (0.19)
RATIOGP	-0.215 (0.53)	0.010 (0.03)	-1.029 (6.08)	-0.446 (0.65)

TABLE 21 (continued)

MAXIMUM LIKELIHOOD DICHOTOMOUS LOGIT EQUATIONS:
CHILDREN WITH A REGULAR SOURCE (t–values in parentheses)

ERLAND	1.404	–2.1E–5	–2.3E–4	–5.0E–4
	(3.59)	(0.06)	(0.76)	(0.91)
PHS_LIM	0.733	0.555	0.194	0.150
	(2.27)	(2.38)	(0.61)	(0.42)
BEDDAYL	0.612	0.548	0.105	–0.056
	(4.48)	(5.97)	(1.12)	(0.51)
HOSP	15.445	0.305	–6.3E–4	–0.329
	(2.48)	(0.95)	(0.00)	(0.82)
CONSTANT	2.874	0.157	1.492	–0.018
	(5.58)	(0.35)	(2.88)	(0.02)
ADJUSTED R–SQ (SRS)	0.269	0.162	0.048	0.093
R–SQ (LSD)	0.035	0.052	0.007	0.010
n	1,161	1,161	1,161	1,161
CHI–SQ	399.14	294.13	87.39	103.80

Notes:

1. The t–values were calculated after adjustments for the complex sample design. The critical t–ratio at the 5 percent level of significance is 1.96 for a two–tailed test.

2. R–SQ (SRS) refers to the proportion of variance explained under simple random sampling assumptions. R–SQ (CSD) refers to the proportion of variance explained when the complex sample design is taken into account. The second value is much lower because of the restrictions on the degrees of freedom based on the number of PSUs.

3. E(integer) signifies that the value should be multiplied by the indicated power of ten.

Source: 1980 National Medical Care Utilization and Expenditure Survey.

TABLE 22

WEIGHTED LEAST SQUARES REGRESSION EQUATIONS:
CHILDREN WITH A REGULAR SOURCE (t-values in parentheses)

Variable	LOGALLMH (Eq. 13)	LOGALLMH (Eq. 14)	LOGPRVMH (Eq. 15)	LOGPRVMH (Eq. 16)
REALAGE	-0.112	-0.110	-0.104	-0.103
	(5.89)	(5.71)	(4.28)	(4.23)
AGESQ	0.006	0.006	0.006	0.006
	(5.18)	(4.90)	(4.42)	(4.39)
RACE3	-0.072	-0.078	-0.093	-0.101
	(1.12)	(1.27)	(1.28)	(1.39)
EDSTAT	-0.163	-0.145	-0.080	-0.082
	(3.11)	(2.92)	(1.27)	(1.26)
CHILDREN	-0.052	-0.048	-0.023	-0.018
	(2.98)	(2.68)	(1.17)	(0.98)
INCOME	-2.0E-5	-2.2E-5	-3.8E-6	-4.7E-5
	(2.82)	(2.81)	(0.40)	(0.49)
OOPPCT	-0.014	--	-0.01	--
	(4.71)		(2.56)	
PRIVATE	--	-0.018	--	-0.079
		(0.28)		(1.29)
UNINSURE	--	-0.173	--	-0.067
		(2.32)		(0.81)
RSMD	-0.010	-0.038	-0.282	0.268
	(0.17)	(0.63)	(4.28)	(4.11)
TRAVEL	4.2E-4	3.2E-4	-8.1E-5	-2.1E-4
	(0.22)	(0.17)	(0.00)	(0.10)
WAIT	-2.2E-4	-1.5E-4	-4.5E-4	-5.2E-4
	(0.40)	(0.27)	(0.77)	(0.90)
PC_MD	-1.4E-4	-1.3E-4	-9.9E-5	-9.2E-5
	(1.70)	(1.72)	(1.17)	(1.11)
RATIOGP	-0.079	-0.101	-0.117	-0.126
	(0.55)	(0.70)	(0.76)	(0.83)

TABLE 22 (continued)

WEIGHTED LEAST SQUARES REGRESSION EQUATIONS:
CHILDREN WITH A REGULAR SOURCE (t–values in parentheses)

ERLAND	3.1E–4	3.1E–4	–5.4E–5	–4.4E–5
	(3.20)	(3.17)	(0.66)	(0.53)
PHS_LIM	0.399	0.408	0.222	0.229
	(4.92)	(5.10)	(2.45)	(2.52)
BEDDAYL	0.226	0.224	0.175	0.175
	(9.44)	(9.28)	(5.60)	(5.57)
HOSP	0.369	0.363	0.332	0.334
	(3.70)	(3.55)	(2.46)	(2.45)
CONSTANT	1.531	1.543	0.817	0.824
ADJUSTED				
R–SQ (SRS)	0.299	0.293	0.227	0.221
R–SQ (LSD)	0.097	0.093	0.056	0.055
n	848	848	561	561
CHI–SQ	46.74	42.99	15.07	14.89

Notes:

1. The t–values were calculated after adjustments for the
   complex sample design. The critical t–ratio at the
   5 percent level of significance is 1.96 for a two–tailed test.

2. R–SQ (SRS) refers to the proportion of variance explained
   under simple random sampling assumptions. R–SQ (CSD) refers
   to the proportion of variance explained when the complex sample
   design is taken into account. The second value is much lower
   because of the restrictions on the degrees of freedom based on
   the number of PSUs.

3. E(integer) signifies that the value should be multiplied by the
   indicated power of ten.

Source: 1980 National Medical Care Utilization and Expenditure Survey.

a regular source of care continued to have fewer visits overall than Medicaid children with a regular source (LOGALLMH).

Income and Price Elasticities

Table 23 displays the income and price elasticities for children with a regular source. The price elasticity (-0.053) for any type of physician visit (LOGALLMH) is similar to the price elasticity for the total sample (-0.055). For visits to a private physician (LOGPRVMH), however, the price elasticity among those with a regular source was slightly lower than that in the total sample: -0.065 versus -0.081. This would make sense, if those with a regular source have a higher degree of commitment to a specific physician and are more likely than those with no regular source to make return visits or to contact a regular physician if care is needed.

The income elasticity for any type of visit (LOGALLMH) was -0.160. This result is consistent with that reported for the total sample (although a slightly higher magnitude). It would appear, therefore, that the variable INCOME reflects the opportunity cost of a visit, and hence, the indirect cost of a visit. Thus, as income increases, use decreases among low-income children (below 150 percent of the federal poverty level).

COMPARISON OF MEDICAID AND NON-MEDICAID CHILDREN: DETERMINANTS OF USE

Tables 24 and 25 contain the separate equations for the Medicaid and non-Medicaid children. This analysis excludes children who had both Medicaid and private insurance during the year.[7] In addition, this analysis excludes the preventive care equations (PREVALL and PREVPRIV) because of the small sample sizes.[8]

Generally, the child's health status was the most significant determinant of health service use by both Medicaid and non-Medicaid children. The number of bed-days (BEDDAYL) was directly related to the probability and volume of use among Medicaid and non-Medicaid children. The other two measures--perceived health status (PHS_LIM) and a hospitalization in 1980 (HOSP)--were not related to the probability of use but generally were related to the number of visits among Medicaid and non-Medicaid children with at least one visit.

This section highlights the effect of economic factors, community resources, and selected sociodemographic characteristics on physician use by Medicaid and non-Medicaid children.

TABLE 23

INCOME AND PRICE ELASTICITIES FOR CHILDREN WITH A REGULAR
SOURCE OF CARE: LOW–INCOME CHILDREN, UNITED STATES, 1980

	Mean	Elasticity
A. INCOME ELASTICITIES		
LOGALLMH	$8,172	–0.160
LOGPRVMH	$8,446	0.046
B. PRICE ELASTICITIES		
LOGALLMH	3.82	–0.053
LOGPRVMH	4.72	–0.065

Note: Elasticities were calculated based on the income and price
  coefficients from the total sample (Table 22, eq. 13 and 15) and the
  corresponding weighted means for the total sample.

Source: 1980 National Medical Care Utilization and Expenditure Survey.

TABLE 24

MAXIMUM LIKELIHOOD DICHOTOMOUS LOGIT EQUATIONS:
MEDICAID AND NON-MEDICAID CHILDREN (t-values in parentheses)

| | VSTALLMH | | VSTPRVMH | |
| | Medicaid | Non–Medicaid | Medicaid | Non–Medicaid |
Variable	(Eq. 17)	(Eq. 18)	(Eq. 19)	(Eq. 20)
REALAGE	-0.169	-0.191	-0.054	-0.143
	(1.66)	(2.32)	(0.66)	(1.93)
AGESQ	0.006	0.006	0.002	0.007
	(1.08)	(1.39)	(0.46)	(1.74)
RACE3	0.025	-0.345	-0.189	-0.425
	(0.07)	(1.14)	(0.63)	(1.79)
EDSTAT	-0.021	-0.545	-0.283	-0.239
	(0.06)	(2.61)	(1.04)	(1.11)
CHILDREN	-0.167	-0.227	-0.170	-0.314
	(1.83)	(2.47)	(1.72)	(4.38)
INCOME	3.8E-5	-7.5E-5	-1.1E-5	2.0E-5
	(0.77)	(2.54)	(0.24)	(0.67)
MED_PY	0.220	--	0.246	--
	(0.41)		(0.65)	
PRIVATE	--	0.060	--	0.424
		(0.27)		(2.19)
PC_MD	-7.3E-4	1.2E-4	-8.4E-4	-4.0E-4
	(2.08)	(0.23)	(3.20)	(0.83)
RATIOGP	-0.155	-0.338	-0.234	0.743
	(0.21)	(0.66)	(0.36)	(1.13)

TABLE 24 (continued)

MAXIMUM LIKELIHOOD DICHOTOMOUS LOGIT EQUATIONS:
MEDICAID AND NON-MEDICAID CHILDREN (t-values in parentheses)

ERLAND	1.324	1.412	-2.5E-5	-1.5E-4
	(3.22)	(2.81)	(0.73)	(0.27)
PHS_LIM	0.459	0.450	0.422	0.598
	(0.93)	(1.08)	(1.26)	(1.48)
BEDDAYL	0.478	0.659	0.362	0.541
	(1.99)	(5.20)	(2.24)	(5.59)
HOSP	1.269	1.368	0.462	0.451
	(1.56)	(1.25)	(1.10)	(1.12)
CONSTANT	2.396	2.308	1.251	-0.135
	(3.15)	(3.78)	(2.06)	(0.14)
ADJUSTED R-SQ (SRS)	0.204	0.277	0.058	0.091
R-SQ (LSD)	0.022	0.045	0.015	0.023
n	464	722	464	722
CHI-SQ	131.04	277.40	62.98	115.81

Notes:
1. The t-values were calculated after adjustments for the
   complex sample design. The critical t-ratio at the
   5 percent level of significance is 1.96 for a two-tailed test.

2. R-SQ (SRS) refers to the proportion of variance explained
   under simple random sampling assumptions. R-SQ (CSD) refers
   to the proportion of variance explained when the complex sample
   design is taken into account. The second value is much lower
   because of the restrictions on the degrees of freedom based on
   the number of PSUs.

3. E(integer) signifies that the value should be multiplied by the
   indicated power of ten.

Source: 1980 National Medical Care Utilization and Expenditure Survey.

TABLE 25

WEIGHTED LEAST SQUARES REGRESSION EQUATIONS:
MEDICAID AND NON-MEDICAID CHILDREN (t-values in parentheses)

| | LOGALLMH | | LOGPRVMH | |
| | Medicaid | Non-Medicaid | Medicaid | Non-Medicaid |
Variable	(Eq. 21)	(Eq. 22)	(Eq. 23)	(Eq. 24)
REALAGE	-0.113	-0.125	-0.131	-0.092
	(3.58)	(5.16)	(4.42)	(3.01)
AGESQ	0.006	0.007	0.008	0.005
	(3.16)	(4.48)	(4.36)	(3.18)
RACE3	0.008	-0.128	0.050	-0.194
	(0.10)	(1.53)	(0.41)	(2.23)
EDSTAT	-0.152	-0.195	-0.085	-0.161
	(1.48)	(2.87)	(0.69)	(2.51)
CHILDREN	-0.069	-0.043	-0.057	-0.063
	(1.99)	(1.72)	(1.65)	(2.34)
INCOME	-1.4E-5	-1.4E-5	1.1E-5	1.3E-5
	(1.06)	(1.53)	(0.84)	(1.23)
OOPPCT	-0.011	-0.012	-0.014	-0.008
	(0.65)	(3.53)	(0.57)	(2.07)
RSMD	0.186	0.039	0.122	0.014
	(1.05)	(0.37)	(0.62)	(0.10)
RSNONMD	0.115	0.146	-0.225	-0.141
	(0.53)	(1.35)	(0.84)	(1.14)
PC_MD	-1.0E-4	-1.8E-4	-2.2E-5	-8.3E-5
	(1.05)	(1.07)	(0.22)	(0.53)
RATIOGP	-0.135	-0.095	-0.046	-0.095
	(0.53)	(0.53)	(0.14)	(0.62)

TABLE 25 (continued)

WEIGHTED LEAST SQUARES REGRESSION EQUATIONS:
MEDICAID AND NON-MEDICAID CHILDREN (t-values in parentheses)

ERLAND	1.9E-4	4.3E-4	-1.5E-4	3.3E-5
	(1.58)	(1.92)	(1.48)	(0.20)
PHS_LIM	0.439	0.509	0.336	0.342
	(4.12)	(3.51)	(2.14)	(2.49)
BEDDAYL	0.229	0.195	0.229	0.147
	(6.20)	(5.64)	(4.23)	(3.48)
HOSP	0.305	0.608	0.305	0.546
	(2.13)	(5.37)	(1.83)	(3.28)
CONSTANT	1.353	1.437	0.845	0.942
ADJUSTED				
R-SQ (SRS)	0.283	0.331	0.264	0.245
R-SQ (LSD)	0.095	0.119	0.096	0.072
n	351	488	351	488
CHI-SQ	9.92	21.53	12.69	11.95

Notes:
1. The t-values were calculated after adjustments for the
   complex sample design. The critical t-ratio at the
   5 percent level of significance is 1.96 for a two-tailed test.
2. R-SQ (SRS) refers to the proportion of variance explained
   under simple random sampling assumptions. R-SQ (CSD) refers
   to the proportion of variance explained when the complex sample
   design is taken into account. The second value is much lower
   because of the restrictions on the degrees of freedom based on
   the number of PSUs.
3. E(integer) signifies that the value should be multiplied by the
   indicated power of ten.

Source: 1980 National Medical Care Utilization and Expenditure Survey.

Economic Factors

As would be expected, family income (INCOME) was not a significant factor among Medicaid children, since Medicaid is targeted to welfare recipients. Within the non-Medicaid population, income was negatively related to the probability of any visit (VSTALLMH). As discussed previously, the negative income effect is most likely due to the opportunity cost involved in making a visit. Among those non-Medicaid children making at least one visit (LOGALLMH), there were no significant income differences in the number of visits. In addition, income was not a significant factor in the use of private physicians (VSTPRVMH and LOGPRVMH).

With respect to insurance coverage, the separate equations controlled for the effects of having Medicaid part of the year (MED_PY) versus the entire year (Medicaid equations) and the effect of private insurance coverage (PRIVATE) versus no insurance coverage (non-Medicaid equations). Children with Medicaid part of the year (MED_PY) did not have a significantly different probability of a visit (overall or to a private physician) than those covered the full year. Thus, there appears to be no difference between full-year and part-year Medicaid children, after controlling for other factors, especially health status. Furthermore, the percent of total charges paid out-of-pocket (OOPPCT) was not a significant factor in the volume of visits by Medicaid children, most likely because children on Medicaid had very low out-of-pocket payments relative to total charges.

Among non-Medicaid children, those with private insurance (PRIVATE) coverage were more likely to visit a private physician (VSTPRVMH), compared to uninsured children. There were no differences between the two groups in the probability of any contact (VSTALLMH). Unlike for the Medicaid children. the relative price (OOPPCT) of care was significantly and inversely related to the number of visits among users. As would be expected, the price elasticities for uninsured children were greater than for the privately insured children. Thus, health service use by uninsured children was more responsive to changes in price, compared to those who were privately insured.

Community Resources

Community resource variables were not significantly related to the probability or volume of use by non-Medicaid children, whereas they had a significant effect on health service use by Medicaid children. For example among Medicaid children, the availability of primary care physicians (PC_MD) was negatively related to the probability of any visit (VSTALLMH) as well as of a visit to a private physician (VSTPRVMH). As discussed previously, the negative effect may be due to (1) a preference by primary care physicians to treat non-Medicaid (or higher income) children, or (2) the availability of other facilities in high physician density areas. Physician availability was not related to the volume of use by Medicaid children who had any ambulatory care.

The level of Medicaid reimbursement (RATIOGP) did not have a significant effect on any of the four utilization measures. It is unclear whether this nonsignificant result is a function of the measure used or whether the level of Medicaid reimbursement simply is not an important factor in health service use, once other factors are controlled.

The availability of emergency rooms (ERLAND) was significantly related to the probability of a physician visit (VSTALLMH) by Medicaid children. Otherwise, the availability of emergency rooms was not a significant factor in health service use by Medicaid children.

Selected Sociodemographic Characteristics

Educational status of the family was not a significant factor in the probability or volume of use for Medicaid children. In contrast, non-Medicaid children in families with a high school graduate had a higher likelihood of any visit (VSTALLMH), and among those with at least one visit (LOGALLMH and LOGPRVMH) a higher number of visits.

Another difference between the Medicaid and non-Medicaid children was the effect of the number of children in the family (CHILDREN). For those on Medicaid, the number of children had an inverse effect only on the number of visits overall (LOGALLMH). The reverse was true for non-Medicaid children--the number of children had a significant and negative effect on the three other measures. The results related to educational status and the number of children suggest that non-Medicaid children in families with a low educational status or a large number of children face certain constraints that are effectively removed by Medicaid coverage. That is, Medicaid may equalize health service use among those with low/high educational status and many/few children.

DISCUSSION

The preceding analyses have shown that Medicaid coverage has a consistent effect on increasing physician use by low-income children, but in general the effect is not large once other factors are controlled. However, an important effect of Medicaid coverage appears to be increased access to private physicians: Medicaid children had a higher probability of visiting a private physician compared to privately insured and uninsured children.

Price was a significant determinant of the number of visits, with use falling as the relative price increased. (As discussed in Chapter 4, the amount paid out-of-pocket is related to the type of insurance coverage.) The price elasticities for the total sample were less than -0.10. The responsiveness to price was greatest among non-Medicaid children (especially those who were uninsured) and those with a relative price above zero. In summary, the price elasticities for the total sample were generally lower than estimates from other studies, while the estimates for the non-Medicaid population as well as estimates excluding children with no out-of-pocket charges fell within the range from other studies.[9] Given the relatively low price elasticities within this low-income population, it is not too surprising that Medicaid coverage had a small effect on the number of visits among those with at least one visit.

Acton (1976) reported that the time involved in a physician visit was an indirect cost, and acted as a rationing device much the same as money price affects use. In the present study, travel time was not a significant factor, but little variation was reported in average travel time. In the case of waiting time, the likelihood of seeing a private physician decreased as waiting time increased. The present study included a direct measure of the relative price of care, whereas Acton relied on travel and waiting times as measures of the "cost" of a visit, in the absence of any price information. In general, therefore, this study found little direct evidence that time functions as a rationing device. However, there was indirect evidence that higher opportunity costs may lead to lower use. Within the total sample, the number of visits among children with at least one visit decreased as income rose. This inverse relationship between income and use was also demonstrated in the separate analysis of non-Medicaid children.

As expected, age and health status were consistently important factors in the use of physicians' services, although the use of preventive care was unrelated to the child's health status. Some previous studies (such as Colle and Grossman, 1978) found that the likelihood of preventive care use was higher among those in excellent or good health, suggesting a substitution of preventive for curative care. This study found the opposite. Children in fair or poor health or with an activity limitation were more likely (but not significantly more likely) to receive preventive care than children in excellent or good health.

Three characteristics of the family--race, educational status, and number of children--were significantly related to some or all of the utilization measures, in the equations for the total sample. Interestingly in the separate equations for the Medicaid and non-Medicaid children, these family characteristics generally had a significant effect on health service use by non-Medicaid children but no by Medicaid children. This would suggest that such constraints are removed, to a large extent, by Medicaid coverage.

The findings regarding race are of interest, because they indicate that significant racial differences exist only in the likelihood of seeing a private physician, and then only in the non-Medicaid population. Colle and Grossman

(1978) also found that there were no race differences in the number of visits or the probability of preventive care use. They did find a significant difference in the probability of any use, while this study found a difference only in the use of private physicians.

The two groups of variables with unexpectedly weak results were the community resource and organizational variables. In general, having a regular source of care--either a physician's office or other place--was not associated with a greater number of visits, compared to those with no regular source. This finding makes sense, given that this comparison was made for children with at least one visit. Having a regular source may be more important in the decision to make the initial contact, rather than in the number of visits.

Physician availability was negatively associated with the likelihood of a visit to a private physician. Although unexpected, three possible explanations were offered. It is possible that in physician-dense areas, physicians are competing for the higher-income privately insured patients, or that these areas have an abundance of other types of resources (OPDs, ERs, or public health clinics). Alternatively, the physician-population ratio, measured at the county level, may overstate the availability of private physicians in inner-city areas where the low-income population is concentrated. In the separate equations for Medicaid and non-Medicaid children, this negative effect of physician availability was found only for the Medicaid children.

Much interest has focused on the effect of Medicaid reimbursement levels on health service use. Provider-level studies have shown that physician willingness to participate in Medicaid is highly dependent on the level of Medicaid fees. A recent state-level study on determinants of expenditures per recipient for physicians' services found that states with a fixed-fee schedule (and generally lower fees) had lower expenditures per recipient (Paringer, 1984). The present study, using the child as the unit of analysis, obtained nonsignificant results on the reimbursement variable. Demand characteristics of the child and family were far more important than supply variables. It is unclear whether this is a statistical artifact due to the unit of analysis and aggregation (state, provider, person), or whether at the individual level demand characteristics actually are the motivating factors and supply characteristics are secondary.

The final resource variable, the availability of emergency rooms, was positively associated with the probability and volume of use and reflects the tendency among low-income children (especially those on Medicaid) to use emergency rooms. Holahan (1984) and Hadley (1981) suggested that states with low levels of physician participation in Medicaid may have higher levels of use of outpatient departments. An implication of the present study may be that low physician participation in Medicaid results in the higher use of emergency rooms. Additional support for this implication is that the availability of emergency rooms is inversely related to the use of private physicians (although this relationship is not significant). Despite the higher cost and fragmentation of care, emergency rooms remain an important source of care for low-income children.

A final remark about the regression analysis presented in this chapter concerns the "fit" of the model to the data. The F-ratio measures the overall fit of the model for the volume equations, while the chi-square measure applies to the probability equations. For all equations, the F-ratio or chi-square was significant at the 0.001 level. The R-square measures the proportion of variance explained by the variables. Using simple random sampling assumptions the R-square ranged from about 0.05 in the preventive equations to as much as 0.30 in the volume equations. Obviously, a substantial proportion of the variance remains unexplained; however, the explanatory power tends to be lower in individual demand studies than in studies at an aggregate level because of the randomness of physician utilization. In addition, the variables are subject to a high degree of measurement error. Overall, the regression equations in the present study have relatively high explanatory power, compared to other individual demand studies.

NOTES

1. A supplementary regression analysis was conducted including low-income children in three "pure" insurance categories: (1) Medicaid coverage the entire year and no other coverage; (2) private insurance coverage the entire year and no other coverage; and (3) no insurance the entire year. The purpose was to examine further the effect of Medicaid and private insurance.

The findings of this analysis were similar to those reported for the full sample. In general, Medicaid coverage had relatively little measurable effect on physician use, once other factors were controlled. However, children who were privately insured the entire year had a lower probability of visits to a private physician (VSTPRVMH), compared to Medicaid children. Additionally, uninsured children with at least one physician visit had fewer visits (LOGALLMH) than Medicaid children.

The price elasticity for the full sample and the subgroup of those with "pure" coverage were similar (in absolute terms). The price elasticity for private physician visits (LOGPRVMH) in the total sample was -0.081 versus -0.086 in the subsample. The price elasticities for total visits (LOGALLMH) were -0.055 and -0.047, for the full sample and the subsample, respectively.

2. As discussed in Chapter 3, the standard errors of the regression coefficient derived through logistic regression were inflated by the design effect obtained in PROC SURREGR (an RTI procedure that runs under SAS). This adjustment method may cause some coefficients that were significant in the unadjusted logistic regression equations to become nonsignificant at the 0.05 level. Specifically, PRIVATE became nonsignificant in VSTALLMH, PREVALL, and PREVPRIV. UNINSURE became nonsignificant in VSTALLMH.

3. The predicted utilization figures were derived by multiplying the coefficients from the regression equations by the mean values for the full sample, adjusting the assumptions about health status and insurance coverage. The coefficients for both the probability and volume equations were generated by weighted least squares regression.

4. The predicted number of visits, according to age, was calculated based on the coefficients in Table 19 (eq. 6) and the weighted means for the children with at least one visit. Then the antilogarithm was taken to obtain the predicted number of visits. The predicted number of visits according to age are:

Age	Number	Age	Number	Age	Number
1	4.8	7	3.2	13	3.3
2	4.3	8	3.1	14	3.4
3	4.0	9	3.1	15	3.7
4	3.7	10	3.1	16	3.9
5	3.5	11	3.1	17	4.2
6	3.3	12	3.2		

5. A more sensitive unit of measurement for physician availability may be the census tract or market area. Physician data are not routinely available at this unit of analysis, nor are individual identifiers usually available at these levels.

6. The coefficient on RATIOGP in VSTPRVMH is clearly nonsignificant, although prior to adjustment of the standard error, the coefficient was significant at the 0.10 level ($p = 0.0685$). This "discrepancy" has important policy implications for the use of private physicians' services. As noted in the text, the likelihood of a visit to a private physician was inversely related to physician availability (PC_MD). However, the positive sign on RATIOGP would suggest that the likelihood of such a visit may increase as the level of Medicaid reimbursement rises. Furthermore, the availability of emergency rooms (ERLAND) was negatively related to private physician use, but this was not significant. This would mean that private physician use is higher in counties with lesser access to emergency rooms (e.g., rural areas), although this result is not significant.

7. The analyses are based on the following numbers of children:

Measure of use	Medicaid	Non-Medicaid
VSTALLMH/VSTPRVMH	464	722
LOGALLMH	351	488
LOGPRVMH	232	316

8. The use of preventive care is not analyzed in this section because of the exceedingly small numbers of children with such a visit in 1980:

Measure of use	Medicaid	Non-Medicaid
PREVALL	94/464	104/722
PREVPRIV	45/464	57/722

9. According to Farley (1978), "The consensus seems to be that the own money price elasticity of demand for physician services is between -0.1 and -0.3."

Chapter 6

IMPLICATIONS FOR FINANCIAL
ACCESS AND SERVICE DELIVERY

This study has attempted to understand the effect of Medicaid on physician use by low-income children. The policy implications of this study fall into two main categories: the implications of Medicaid and private insurance coverage for improving financial access; and the implications for improving service delivery. Before discussing the policy implications, the context and limitations of the study will be described.

CONTEXT AND LIMITATIONS
OF THIS STUDY

This study uses data collected in calendar year 1980. Since 1980, many changes have taken place in the financing and delivery of health services to both poor and nonpoor populations for publicly and privately-paid health care. For example, many firms have sought to contain the cost of private health insurance by reducing benefits and/or increasing copayments. Additionally, preferred provider arrangements have been negotiated by private insurers as cost-containment mechanisms.

The state-administered Medicaid programs have also experienced retrenchment--in benefits, eligibility, and reimbursement. The following quote is an excellent summary of the important changes that have taken place in the 50 Medicaid programs from 1981 to 1983 (Intergovernmental Health Policy Project, 1983):

> Nineteen Eighty-One can be characterized generally as a period of moderate programs and severe retrenchment on the part of many state Medicaid programs and severe retrenchment for a few. For example, more than 30 states took at least one action that resulted in reducing or

eliminating either one or more services, eligibility groups or provider payments.

Although in 1982 most states continued to encounter serious funding problems, the nature and scope of the states' cost-containment efforts differed significantly from the year before. For the most part, 1982 simply did not bring about the same volume or severity of program limitations as witnessed during 1981. Perhaps the most striking difference between the two years is that, even in the face of continued fiscal stress, a substantial number of states acted in 1982 to add new services, reinstate previously eliminated benefits, lift existing restrictions on access, or even increase payments to providers. Also in contrast to 1981, 1982 marked the beginning of a gradual shift in the focus of cost-containment activities away from the traditional short-term strategies, e.g., limitations on eligibility and services, reductions in provider payments, etc., to a concentration on more long-range, structural reforms in the organization, financing and delivery of Medicaid services.

The changes described above occurred (for the most part) after the data on which this study is based were collected. This may limit the generalizability of the study findings presented in Chapters 4 and 5. On the other hand, to the extent that the turbulence experienced in 1981 and 1982 has settled, the findings should still be relevant.

A strength of this study is that the findings apply to the national level, rather than one state or city. This may also be a limitation, given that the Medicaid program varies from state to state and the commitment to serving the low-income population also varies across localities. Therefore, different findings might be expected in a state or local-level study.

Another limitation of this study is that the dependent variables do not measure the necessity or appropriateness of use. For this reason, it is not clear that "more use is better." Thus, to say that Medicaid children have more visits overall or a higher likelihood of seeing a private physician should not be interpreted to mean the policies should necessarily strive to equalize physician use among Medicaid and non-Medicaid children, regardless of need. Rather, as was pointed out in the introduction to this study, the goal should be equity in health service use. Future research is required to assess the appropriateness of health service use by low-income children, with an emphasis on differences according to insurance coverage.

IMPLICATIONS FOR IMPROVING
FINANCIAL ACCESS

The regression results in Chapter 5 revealed that Medicaid coverage had an important but not overwhelming effect on physician use. In all cases, Medicaid children had a higher probability or volume of use than non-Medicaid children. This difference was significant in two cases. First, it appears that Medicaid offered a "choice" between private physicians and other providers. It may be recalled that Medicaid children had a significantly higher probability of seeing a private physician than children who were uninsured or privately insured. In general, however, the probability of any visit (regardless of setting) did not differ significantly between Medicaid and non-Medicaid children.

Another important effect of Medicaid was on the number of visits among those with at least one visit. Medicaid children made more visits than uninsured children, but not compared to those who were privately insured. By lowering the relative price of a visit, Medicaid coverage led to higher physician use among those making at least one visit. The empirical estimate of the price elasticity of visits with an out-of-pocket charge was -0.211. In other words, a 50 percent decrease in the relative price would result in a 10 percent increase in use. Applying this estimate to the average use of uninsured children with at least one visit, a 50 percent reduction in the relative price would result in an increase from 2.8 to 3.1 visits, on average. Thus, because the average number of visits in a given year is relatively low, the expected increase in use under CHAP is expected to be relatively low. Therefore, a policy to expand Medicaid eligibility to low-income uninsured children may be expected to have a relatively low "social cost," that is, the cost of services resulting from a higher demand. However, the "shifted cost" could be somewhat higher, if services paid for out-of-pocket or by other third-party payers (or uncompensated care) are paid by the Medicaid program, as a result of expanded Medicaid eligibility.

This study also found that children who were on Medicaid part of the year tended to be in poorer health than children on Medicaid the full year. Consequently, the part-year Medicaid children were higher users of physicians' services than other children. A reasonable policy option is to target a "medically needy" program to uninsured or underinsured children in states that do not cover the medically needy under Medicaid. Such a program would extend Medicaid to a segment of the poverty population above the states' financial eligibility criteria without increasing the costs to the Medicaid program prohibitively. It was demonstrated that physician use by low-income children is not highly price sensitive, and more importantly, that physician use was primarily motivated by the child's health status.

This study also has implications for the financial access of privately insured low-income children. The low-income children covered by private health insurance may have lower use of private physicians' services, in part, because of the limited scope of benefits covered by their health insurance policies. Furthermore, income, educational status, and number of children may be important factors in health service use by the privately insured due to the "opportunity cost" of taking a child to the doctor.

This group had much narrower benefits for ambulatory care than for inpatient care, with coverage generally for inpatient hospital care (86 percent) and inpatient physician visits (84 percent), but less frequently for office visits to physicians (44 percent), and rarely for dental visits (18 percent).

In this context, it is not surprising that privately insured low-income children had a lower probability of visiting a private physician than Medicaid children. However, among those with at least one visit to a private physician, there was no difference in the number of visits according to insurance coverage. Those making one or more visits are most likely the children with some coverage for office visits (or else, individual arrangements with a private physician). The children with no coverage for office visits may be considered worse off than Medicaid children, and perhaps, in terms of financial access to private physicians, they may be equivalent to uninsured children. At the very least, they are underinsured. Even those with coverage for office visits but with large deductibles effectively may not have coverage if the level of the deductible results in full payment for the few visits made by the majority of the children each year. These problems may be compounded for the 8 percent of the low-income children who were privately insured part of the year and uninsured the remainder of the year.

For children with a narrow scope of benefits, the underinsured, Fullerton (1982) suggested that states could mandate a minimum set of private health insurance benefits for children. State mandates are common in the areas of substance abuse, mental health, and newborn care, among others. Obviously, coverage for physician office visits is an area that many children (especially the low-income) lack. It might be recalled from Chapter 4 that privately insured children made an extremely high proportion of visits to outpatient departments. Mandating office visit coverage could be justified on the basis that it may shift the locus of care from costly hospital-based facilities to less costly physicians' offices. Furthermore, an argument could be made that office-based physicians provide more continuous care than hospital facilities and tend to hospitalize less often (Fleming and Jones, 1983). These factors too, may lead to lower program costs for private insurance companies.

The second area in which privately insured low-income children may face an economic barrier to care is in the opportunity cost for a parent (or other adult) to take time off from work to visit the doctor. The negative income effect was unexpected, although plausible. In minimum-wage positions, sick leave is less generous or even non-existent; furthermore, it frequently cannot be used to take care of a sick child; and finally, advance sick leave may not be available to care for a seriously ill or hospitalized child. In such cases, a parent may lose a half or full day's wages, or at worst, risk losing a job when substantial sick leave is required. The results of this study suggest that increasing the availability of sick leave among employed, low-income parents might alleviate the inverse relationship between income and physician use. However, this may not be feasible in some occupations.

The negative income effect should be explored further using data from other data sets. If this finding is confirmed, there may be evidence of a "welfare effect," that is, an inverse relationship between employment status and child health use, within the low-income population.

IMPLICATIONS FOR IMPROVING
SERVICE DELIVERY

The previous section was concerned with improving financial access to physicians' services in general. This section addresses the question of "access to what services." Although Medicaid increased the likelihood of a private physician visit, the use of hospital-based providers--outpatient departments (OPDs) and emergency rooms (ERs)--was extremely high. Over one-third of the Medicaid children visited an emergency room during 1980 and one-fourth visited an outpatient department. Thirty percent of the visits by Medicaid children were to ERs or OPDs. The figures were comparable for non-Medicaid low-income children.

As Chapter 4 discussed, hospital-based facilities are more costly than physicians' offices or freestanding clinics. On average, emergency room charges ($77.21) were more than three times the charges for office and clinic visits ($22.09 and $21.06, respectively). The average charge for outpatient department visits was double ($44.86). (These amounts are self-reported charges for visits by low-income children that had a charge.) These estimates are remarkably similar to figures from Henderson and Hannon (1983); in California, hospital OPD visits cost $36.92 per visit; nationally, a physician's group practice visit cost $22.17 per visit.

The policy recommendation that follows from these data is not immediately apparent. On the one hand, hospital-based ambulatory care is more expensive than care provided in physicians' offices or freestanding clinics. On the other hand, the product in hospital settings may differ from nonhospital settings. To the extent that hospital outpatient departments are providing more specialized care or even more comprehensive primary care (e.g., social services, referral and follow-up), the higher cost may be warranted.

Lion and Williams (1983) assessed the effect of case-mix differences on visit costs in two settings (hospital OPDs and physician group practices). They concluded, "Roughly a fifth of the cost differential--no small amount but far less than has been previously supposed--is found to be due to either medical or social case mix using the most optimistic assumptions."

In a separate but related study, Henderson and Hannon (1983) found that OPD visits were more costly for two reasons: (1) higher salary costs, including more personnel, higher salaries, and a different mix of personnel; and (2) the presence of "noncounterpart" costs (i.e., hospital overhead costs not present in a physicians' group practice), such as research and education, cafeteria costs, security, inpatient support, and social services.

This evidence would suggest that OPDs are providing a different product, although not necessarily a better one. Where a pediatric primary care project has been developed, frequently in conjunction with a family practice or pediatric residency, the hospital or a satellite neighborhood clinic obviously is an appropriate primary care provider. Otherwise, emergency rooms and pediatric or general medical clinics in hospital outpatient departments tend to be inappropriate sources of routine child health care.

A challenge facing policymakers is to reorient users from hospital facilities to physicians' offices or health clinics, especially in communities with no hospital-based primary care projects. Two strategies could be employed, either separately or jointly, to (1) alter the relative price of a visit depending on the setting; or (2) place the provider at financial risk for the use of multiple providers. Altering the relative price of a visit can be accomplished by imposing a copayment for more costly care (e.g., nonurgent care in ERs and OPDs). If families are at all sensitive to price, the charge may result in a shift to less costly settings, such as physicians' offices or health clinics. Otherwise, the copayment would defray the cost of the visit. To ensure that necessary care is not foregone, an adequate supply of non-hospital providers must be available. Previous research has found that higher Medicaid fees are associated with lower demand for outpatient care.

This study found indirect evidence of that phenomenon. First, physician availability was negatively related to the probability of private physician use, suggesting a preference by providers for higher-income patients or a preference by consumers for non-office-based providers. Higher reimbursements might stimulate office-based physicians to care for Medicaid children, although this is not necessarily the case. The decision to accept Medicaid patients is a function of many other considerations besides monetary concerns.

The second piece of evidence regarding supply-side factors is that the probability and volume of overall physician use is strongly related to the availability of emergency rooms. In addition, there is an inverse relationship between physician availability and overall use (although this relationship is not significant after the complex sample design is taken into account). Perhaps children are using emergency rooms rather than private physicians, despite the availability of private physicians, because of the low level of Medicaid fees and the greater convenience of emergency rooms. (Furthermore, anecdotal information suggests that hospital-based providers are perceived to be of higher quality than private physicians.)

It is recognized that this evidence is indirect, yet this matter bears further exploration in view of the significantly higher use by low-income children of emergency rooms and outpatient departments (compared to nonpoor children). According to Holahan (1984), "National Medicaid data has shown that while physician payments grew little, if at all, in real terms in the late 1970's, hospital outpatient care grew at about 22.0 percent per year."

A concurrent or alternative policy option is to establish a "gatekeeper" system of care. In such a system, prior authorization must be obtained before visiting an OPD or ER. Under capitation, the provider is placed at some level of financial risk. Whether combined with a copayment mechanism such as that described above, or alone, more appropriate utilization of inpatient and outpatient hospital care is encouraged.

Demonstration projects for primary care networks, a form of a "gatekeeper" system, were in effect in 21 states as of June 1984; however, rigorous evaluation has not yet been conducted with respect to cost, utilization, access, and quality of care (Intergovernmental Health Policy Project, 1984). Although they have great promise on a conceptual level, previous experience with serving Medicaid recipients in prepaid systems of care, such as health maintenance organizations has not been altogether positive (Ashcraft and Berki, 1983). The Medi-Cal experience in the mid-1970s is a haunting example of the fraud and abuse that may result from Medicaid "mills." Furthermore, despite the flexibility provided by the Omnibus Budget Reconciliation Act of 1981, restricting freedom-of-choice may create insurmountable administrative problems for providers and state agencies (Spitz, 1982).

In summary, the results have implications for two "access-related" issues. First, financial access to physicians' services can be increased by expanding Medicaid eligibility to uninsured low-income children and by improving private health insurance benefits among the underinsured. Second, the use of less costly sources of care may enhance the appropriateness of use. Although Medicaid appears to offer a "choice" between private physicians and other providers, outpatient hospital use is still extremely high in this population, as well as among non-Medicaid low-income children. Shifting the locus of care from more costly to less costly settings can be accomplished either by altering the relative price of outpatient hospital care, or by placing providers at greater financial risk for inappropriate use of hospital-based ambulatory care, or a combination of the two strategies.

SUMMARY OF MULTIVARIATE UTILIZATION STUDIES

A. Studies of the Pediatric Population

Reference	Purpose of Study	Scope of Sample	Method of Analysis	Measures of utilization	Major Findings
Colle and Grossman 1978	To understand the determinants of physician utilization by preschool children	1971 household interview of a national prob. sample; n = 839 children ages 1-5	Maximum likelihood dichotomous logit; ordinary least squares	Prob. of MD contact; prob. of prev. exam; number of office visits to MDs in private practice; average quality of visits (measured by MD specialty)	The two basic forces in pediatric use were family size and mother's schooling; number of children in a family was inversely related to all four types of use, while mother's schooling was positively related to the probability of MD contact and a prev. exam, but negatively related to the number of visits; in addition, family income was positively related to all four measures; Medicaid and welfare increased the prob. of MD contact and of a prev. exam, but significant differences remained for number and quality of private office visits; number of MDs per capita had no effect on the number of visits but positively affected the other types of use.

Reference	Purpose of Study	Scope of Sample	Method of Analysis	Measures of utilization	Major Findings
Dutton 1978	To explore alternative hypotheses concerning the low use of health services by the poor	1970-71 household interview in two areas in Washington, D.C. n = 681 families, 1,435 children under age 12; primarily black	Stepwise multiple regression	Frequency of children's checkups; prob. of any visits to usual provider in last six months, by child	A positive income trend remained after controlling for demographic, illness, family structure, and socioeconomic factors; income differences in prev. care use were "explained" by health attitudes and type of health care system used; however, even after controlling for attitudes and system type, the likelihood of any type of visit still varied significantly by income.
Dutton 1979	To systematically compare the impact of five different delivery system types on the use of ambulatory care	Same as Dutton 1978	Ordinary least squares	Same as Dutton 1978, in addition, average number of follow-up visits per condition per child	Hospital OPDs, ERs and public clinics (sources used primarily by the poor) had the lowest rate of patient-initiated use and contained structural and financial barriers to use; the PPCP system had the fewest barriers, high prev. use, and did not differ significantly in MD-initiated use; the FFS system had a lower rate of patient-initiated use but higher rate of MD-initiated use.

Reference	Purpose of Study	Scope of Sample	Method of Analysis	Measures of utilization	Major Findings
Goldman and Grossman 1978	To investigate the nature of quantity-quality substitution in the demand for pediatric care	1965-66 interviews with mothers of infants and preschoolers in two health districts in the Bronx, New York; data collection on MDs identified by the mothers; n = 1,687	Two-stage least squares	Annual number of pediatric office visits to MDs in private practice; average quality per visit	As income and quality-adjusted price increased, the ratio of quality to quantity declined; as the fixed cost of a visit increased, quantity decreased and quality increased; the quantity of visits was more responsive to a change in the fixed cost of a visit than to a change in the quality-adjusted price; demand for private pediatric visits was found to be very sensitive to income.
Gortmaker 1981	To determine the extent to which Medicaid children are receiving good quality care, as well as extent to which providers accept Medicaid recipients	1977 household survey in Flint, Michigan and surrounding Genesee County; n = 3,072 children	Difference between two means, unadjusted and adjusted by multiple regression	Mean number of illness-related MD visits; percent with no previous checkup in previous year; percent with no MD visits in previous year; percent with no MD identified as regular source of care	Adjusting for socioeconomic and health status, more Medicaid children had a prev. exam or any MD contact within the previous year (compared to non-Medicaid children); however, Medicaid children were more likely not to identify an MD as a regular source of care; significant differences were not found with respect to the mean number of illness-related MD visits or the percent having a pediatrician as the regular source.

Reference	Purpose of Study	Scope of Sample	Method of Analysis	Measures of utilization	Major Findings
Inman 1976	To estimate demand functions for curative and prev. child health care	Same as Dutton 1978; n=880 working mothers and 812 nonworking mothers with children age 6 months to 12 years	Ordinary least squares	Number of prev. checkups per child per year; number of MD visits within the previous year for ear/nose/throat (ENT) diseases	Time cost found to be one of the most significant determinants of utilization; time cost elasticity higher for non-working mothers than working mothers; price elasticities were generally under 0.15 in absolute value; income elasticity estimated at about 0.16 for nonworking mothers and 0.25 for working mothers; older children, children from larger families, and children with a history of colds or ear problems used more care.
Tessler 1980	To separate out the effects of birth order and family size on children's use of MD services	1973 household interviews with families in PPCP and alternative FFS plans in Milwaukee, Wisconsin; n=587 families, 1,665 children	Ordinary least squares	Prob. of aggregate MD utilization; prob. of prev. care use in the previous year	Birth order and family size maintained independent and statistically significant effects on both measures of MD use; the effect of birth order was stronger for prev. exams than for aggregate use; supports the view that use is a socially learned response, given higher rates of use among first-borns than among later-borns.

Reference	Purpose of Study	Scope of Sample	Method of Analysis	Measures of utilization	Major Findings
Tessler and Mechanic 1978	To examine factors affecting pediatric utilization in a PPCP, with special emphasis on the mother's level of psychological distress	1973 household interview survey and medical records review of PPCP enrollees; n = 175 mothers, 336 children under age 12	Stepwise multiple regression	Prob. and number of MD visits; prob. and number of mother-initiated MD visits	Child's age and number of chronic problems were the significant determinants of the number of visits (total and mother-initiated); the prob. of both types of visits was negatively related to the child's age and race and positively related to the mother's "propensity to seek care for children," mother's level of psychological distress was a factor in the prob. of use among white children and the number of visits among children with at least one MD visit.
Wan and Gray 1978	To determine the relative importance of social and access factors on the use of prev. care among pre-school children	1975 community health survey of residents in five urban NHC service areas; n = 2,063 children ages 0 to 5	Multiple classification analysis	Prob. of prev. exam in previous year	Social class, type of regular source of care, and type of health insurance were significantly related to the use of prev. services among preschool children.

Reference	Purpose of Study	Scope of Sample	Method of Analysis	Measures of utilization	Major Findings
Wolfe 1980	To clarify some of the differences in children's use of medical care, especially by type of provider seen	1975 community health survey in Rochester, New York; n = 814 children, ages 1 to 11	Logit analysis; ordinary least squares	Prob. of MD use in previous year; number of visits for those with at least one visit; percent of total visits, by type of provider	Health status, age, family size, and median tract income were significant determinants of the prob. of MD use; number of visits was a function of health status and age; type of provider seen was associated with income, race, marital status, family size, type of insurance, and median tract income.

B. Studies of the General Population

Reference	Purpose of Study	Scope of Sample	Method of Analysis	Measures of Utilization	Major Findings
Acton 1976	To assess the role of travel and waiting times in the demand for health care among the urban poor, distinguishing between public and private care	1968 household interview survey in two NHC service areas in Brooklyn, New York; about 1,200 households completed survey	Tobit estimation technique	Number of MD visits to hospital OPD of public clinic; number of private office visits	Time prices filled the role of money prices as out-of-pocket expenditures declined; travel time price elasticity was greater for public outpatient care (-0.6 to -1.0) than for private out-patient care (-0.25 to -0.36); effect of waiting time on demand less than effect of travel time; health status variables were the most consistent predictors of demand; nonwhites and the less educated substituted public for private care; large household size reduced the use of both public and private care.
Andersen and Aday 1978	To assess differences in access to medical care, based on predisposing, enabling, and need characteristics	1976 national prob. sample of the noninstitutional population, as well as oversampling of selected groups, n = 7,655 (excluding infants)	Path analysis	Number of face-to-face (home and office) MD visits in the previous year	Age and illness variables were the major determinants of number of visits, suggesting that the health system was relatively equitable; however, availability of regular source of care was also an important (and mutable) factor.

Reference	Purpose of Study	Scope of Sample	Method of Analysis	Measures of Utilization	Major Findings
Andersen and Benham 1970	To measure and assess some factors which influence the relationship between use and family income	1964 national prob. sample of the noninstitutional population, n = 2,167 families	Multiple regression	MD expenditures: charges incurred by families for MD services during the year; MD use: "quantity" of MD services weighted by standard prices	The observed income elasticity for MD expenditures was heavily influenced by such other components as price, quality, demographic characteristics, and use of prev. care; the observed income elasticity was higher than the permanent income elasticity for MD expenditures; the permanent income elasticity increased and became significant when illness level was introduced; permanent income elasticities were always greater for MD expenditures than for MD use.
Berki and Ashcraft 1979	To identify differences in determinants of ambulatory utilization, for both illness and prev. visits	Interviews with employees and dependents from a single firm, who had HMO or BC/BS coverage; n = 560 adults	Ordinary least squares	Number of illness-related visits; number of prev. visits	Predictors of illness and prev. visits different considerably; number of chronic and acute conditions were the strongest predictors of illness visits; lack of usual source of care was associated with fewer visits of both kinds, price was a factor in illness but not prev. use; an increase in prev. visits was associated with fewer illness visits; the number of hospital days was positively related to the number of illness visits; HMO membership was associated with more prev. visits.

Reference	Purpose of Study	Scope of Sample	Method of Analysis	Measures of Utilization	Major Findings
Davis and Reynolds 1976	To explore differences in use among those receiving welfare and other low income persons not on welfare	1969 National Health Interview Survey; n = 3,163 welfare recipients	Tobit estimation technique	Number of MD visits in the two weeks prior to the interview	Health status variables were highly significant in explaining utilization in the two groups; at all levels of health status, the welfare recipients received substantially more services than other low income persons (adjusting for other variables); females 17-44 on welfare had higher use than those not on welfare; family size was a greater constraint on the welfare group; black Medicaid recipients had lower use rates than whites; however, blacks received more medical care with Medicaid than without.
Hershey, Luft, and Gianaris 1975	To evaluate alternative specifications of utilization models	1972 household survey in Livingston, California, n = 299 families, 1,010 persons	Multiple regression	Total number of MD visits in the previous year (excluding inpatient visits); number of patient-initiated visits; prob. of at least one visit to MD in previous year; prob. of prev. exam in previous year	Health status measures and usual source of care measures were important in predicting all measures of utilization; health status was more important in predicting the number versus the prob. of visits; education level was important only in predicting prev. checkups, while income was a factor in patient-initiated and prev. visits; travel time, ethnicity and attitude were insignificant.

Reference	Purpose of Study	Scope of Sample	Method of Analysis	Measures of Utilization	Major Findings
Kronenfeld 1978b	To determine the influence of number of "provider affiliations" on MD use	1974 Rhode Island health survey; n = 1,329 persons	Stepwise multiple regression; partial correlation	Number of ambulatory care visits to MD	Including data on provider affiliations (i.e., number of providers with whom the respondent had a "relationship") yielded a higher percent of explained variance (40 %) than previous research; the two most important predictors were number of affiliations and number of conditions, followed by income (negative) and Medicaid/Medicare coverage (positive).
Kronenfeld 1980	To elaborate on the relationship between ambulatory use and provider variables	Same as Kronenfeld 1978b	Multiple classification analysis	Same as Kronenfeld 1978b	The most important explanatory variable was need, represented by number of conditions while the provider variables were second in importance (i.e., number of affiliations and specialty and type of affiliations), number of disability days was third; the more complex the pattern of use (in terms of number and type of affiliations) the greater the use.
Lairson and Swint 1978	To test an economic framework of demand for prev. care in a PPCP	1969-70 household survey and medical record review of a 5% sample of Kaiser (Portland) PPCP; n = 3,892	Zero-one regression; ordinary least squares	Prob. of prev. visit during the year; annual number of prev. visits among those with at least one	Prob. of at least one prev. visit was positively related to educational level and being female as well as the quadratic age term; it was negatively related to actual age; the coinsurance level had a negative effect, while income had a positive effect; the only significant determinants of number of prev. visits were family size and age (both negative) and the quadratic age term (positive); health status was insignificant in both equations.

Reference	Purpose of Study	Scope of Sample	Method of Analysis	Measures of Utilization	Major Findings
Rundall and Wheeler 1979	To estimate direct and indirect effect of income on prev. care use	1977 household survey in Washtenaw County, Michigan; n = 781 adults	Path analysis	Estimated annual visit rate for prev. care	Income did not have a significant direct effect on prev. use; the indirect effect through "perceived susceptibility to illness" was positive but weak; having a regular source of care had the strongest indirect effect of income on use.
Salkever 1976	To apply the economic demand model to prev. care use among adults	1968-69 household survey in Baltimore, North Western Vermont, and Saskatchewan, Canada; n = 1,625, 898, and 1,773 respectively; adults over 15	Ordinary least squares	Prob. of obtaining a prev. checkup in previous year	Income had a rather insignificant effect on demand and insurance coverage had a non-monotonic effect (those who paid nothing out-of-pocket had a lower demand than those with some copayment); the most important time cost variables were having a regular physician and having a regular source of care; attitudinal variables were more consistently significant than were financial or physical access factors.
Sharp, Ross, and Cockerham 1983	To examine the relationship between race/education and health attitudes as well as effect of attitudes on MD use	1980 telephone survey in Illinois; n = 618 adults	Path analysis	Total number of MD visits in previous year	Blacks and the less educated were more likely than whites and the better educated to have positive attitudes toward visiting MDs and to think that certain symptoms were serious enough to warrant MD attention; neither attitudes nor symptoms alone affected use--a person must have had a symptom and considered it serious.

Reference	Purpose of Study	Scope of Sample	Method of Analysis	Measures of Utilization	Major Findings
Skinner, German, Shapiro, Chase, and Zauber 1978	To examine the use of ambulatory care among the near poor and consider the influence of different service delivery mechanisms	1974 household survey of adults (ages 18-64) in East Baltimore; primarily black; 3 subsamples; PPCP members (n=544); housing project residents (n=539); community at large (n=497)	Multiple linear regression	Number of ambulatory visits in the previous six months	Health status variables were the strongest predictors of use for all three subsamples; also near poor adults in all three groups used fewer services than Medicaid recipients; HMO enrollment acted to minimize utilization differences between the near poor and Medicaid recipients.
Tanner, Cockerham and Spaeth 1983	To propose a measure of "need" that improves on the measures generally used	1980 telephone survey in Illinois; n=618 adults	Multiple regression	Total number of MD visits in previous year	The proposed measure--respondent-evaluated symptoms (RES)--was an improvement over the global measure of perceived health status (PHS) or the separate measures of number of symptoms and seriousness of symptoms; the effects of sex, race, and education became insignificant when PHS was augmented by other measures of need; including RES as a measure of perceived need raised the adjusted R-squared from 0.113 (PHS alone) to 0.188 (PHS and RES).

Reference	Purpose of Study	Scope of Sample	Method of Analysis	Measures of Utilization	Major Findings
Wan and Soifer 1974	To determine the casual ordering of factors related to MD utilization	1972 community health survey in 5 NY/PA counties; n = 2,168 households	Path analysis	Average annual number of MD visits per person per household	Need for care (represented by percent of household perceiving poor health status and percent responding to illness) was the strongest direct predictor of use; average cost per visit and presence of private insurance coverage were next in importance; the percent of household members who were elderly and percent female were also significantly related to household use.
Wolinsky 1978	To assess Andersen's (1968) framework of health services utilization	1971, 1972, 1973 National Health Interview Survey of the general population; n = 134,502 - 1971 132,891 - 1972 120,493 - 1973	Path analysis	Number of MD visits in past 12 months; interval since last MD visit	As operationalized in this study, the Andersen framework was found to explain very little variance in the two MD utilization measures (R-squared ranged from 0.09 to 0.16); most of explained variance attributable to the illness-morbidity characteristics; recommended future research to modify this casual model.

Appendix 2

THE NMCUES NATIONAL HOUSEHOLD SURVEY

This appendix provides an overview of the sampling, interviewing, weighting, and imputation procedures employed in the National Household Survey (HHS) component of the National Medical Care Utilization and Expenditure Survey (NMCUES). The NMCUES includes two other components--the State Medicaid Household Survey and the Administrative Records Survey--but neither are discussed in this appendix.

SAMPLING PROCEDURES

The sample design for the HHS component of NMCUES consisted of two independently drawn national samples based on similar stratified four-stage area probability designs (NCHS, 1983c). The population of inference is the civilian, noninstitutionalized population living in the U.S. at the beginning of 1980. The sampling was conducted by Research Triangle Institute (RTI) and a subcontractor, the National Opinion Research Center (NORC). The four stages were:

Stage	Description	Number Selected
1	Primary sampling unit (PSU): counties, parts of counties, groups of contiguous counties	135 PSUs; 108 separate primary areas, excluding duplication

2	Secondary sampling unit (SSU): census enumeration districts or block groups	809 SSUs
3	Smaller area segments within each SSU	809 small area segments (one per SSU)
4	Housing units (HUs)	7,596 HUs, 7,244 eligible HUs

In the 7,244 eligible housing units, 6,599 reporting units were interviewed, yielding a response rate of 91 percent in round one, of which 97 percent completed round five. A reporting unit includes "all persons related to each other by blood, marriage, adoption, or foster care status and living in the same dwelling unit" (Mugge, 1984). Unmarried students ages 17 to 22 living away from home were included in the sample when the parent or guardian was included in the sample.

INTERVIEW PROCEDURES

During 1980 and early 1981, each participating reporting unit was interviewed five times, about every three months. The respondent was a household member at least 17 years old, although a proxy respondent was allowed when household members could not respond due to poor health, language barrier, or mental disorder. Interviews were conducted in person, except for the round three and four telephone interviews. The average length ranged from 0.8 hours (round four) to 1.4 hours (round one). Three of the interviews involved cash incentives. (See Table 26.) The interviews revolved around four main survey instruments (Bonham, 1983):

- Control card: A computer-generated instrument providing administrative control of the sample, information to help the interviewer locate and identify sample persons, procedures for determining reporting unit composition, and places to record information required across rounds of interviewing.

- Core questionnaire: The basic interview instrument used during each interview to obtain data about health, health care, charges

TABLE 26

DESCRIPTION OF INTERVIEW FORMAT AND CONTENT: NMCUES NATIONAL HOUSEHOLD SURVEY

Interview Round	Dates of Interview	Form of Interview	Incentive Payment	Average Length of Interview	CONTENT OF INTERVIEWS*			
					CC	CQ	SUPP	SUMM
1	Feb.-Apr. 1980	Face-to-face	$5.00	1.4 hours	X	X	X	-
2	May-July 1980	Face-to-face	$5.00	1.2 hours	X	X	-	X
3	Aug.-Oct. 1980	Telephone	None	1.0 hours	X	X	X	X
4**	Nov.-Dec. 1980	Telephone	None	0.8 hours	X	X	-	X
5	Jan.-Mar. 1981	Face-to-face	$10.00	1.3 hours	X	X	X	X

*Content of interview: CC = control card; CQ = core questionnaire; SUPP = supplements; SUMM = summary; see text for explanation.

**Round 4 interviews were conducted with only two-thirds of the sample: the other one-third (generally interviewed in Round 3 in October) were the first reporting units contacted in Round 5.

for health care, sources of payment, and health insurance coverage.

• Supplements: Sets of questions asked at only one of the interviews; used only in rounds 1, 3, and 5.

• Summary of responses: A computer-generated report containing summary information of previously reported health care, charges for care, sources of payment, and health insurance coverage. It was designed to update information that may not have been available to the respondent at the time the health care was originally reported. Another purpose was to ensure that events were not reported more than once.

Another tool to assist respondent recall was a calendar, on which family members could record medical visits, charges, payments, bed-days, and other health-related events. In addition, each reporting unit was given a folder for copies of bills and receipts to further assist the interviewer.

IMPUTATION PROCEDURES

Separate imputation procedures were developed for attrition nonresponse and item nonresponse. The public use data tape indicates whether a value is based on "real data" or "imputed data," and whether a respondent with "real data" acted as a donor for the statistical imputation of missing data.

In the case of attrition nonresponse--where responses were available for the first interview round, but not in subsequent rounds--data were imputed based on the responses of full-year respondents with similar characteristics. Of the 91,502 records on the medical visit file, 263 (0.5 percent) were imputed due to attrition of originally-responding sample members (NCHS, 1983c).

Among full-year respondents with missing data on specific questionnaire items (as well as those missing rounds at some point in the survey), logical imputation was used whenever possible, that is, when other responses suggested the appropriate response. Otherwise, the missing data were statistically imputed by assigning a value from a responding person with similar characteristics to that of the nonrespondent. The percent imputed varied, depending upon the degree of difficulty encountered in obtaining the data (NCHS, 1983c). Thus, a higher than usual proportion of responses were imputed for data on charges, amounts paid by different sources, and sources of income. For example, 25.9 percent of the total charges on the medical visit file were imputed. However, the total charge response was considered an imputed value if one or more of the component charges was imputed. Specifically for the low-income children in this study's sample, 59 percent of the total charges for physician visits were imputed.

WEIGHTING PROCEDURES

Weights have been constructed to produce national estimates that incorporate nonresponse as well as the 1980 population counts from the decennial census. The "basic sample design weight" was calculated on the basis of the probability of selection across the four stages of sampling. The basic weight reflects the number of units (such as persons or visits) that the sample unit represents in the population of inference. Three adjustments were made to the basic weight. First, an adjustment was made to account for the two independent samples (RTI and NORC) within the NMCUES. The second adjustment was for nonresponse or undercoverage, at the reporting unit level. The adjustment factor was based on the number of RUs within 63 cells (reflecting age, race, and type of householder, and size of RU), in relation to the estimated number of RUs in each cell, according to the March 1980 Current Population Survey.

Finally, an adjustment of the person-level weights was made through post-stratification, based on data from the 1980 Census of Population. This final post-stratification brings the sample estimates into agreement with the size of the noninstitutionalized, civilian population in 1980 according to age, sex, and race subgroups. The national estimate for any one of these cells from the sample will agree precisely with the July 1, 1980 estimate published by the Bureau of the Census. Thus, the number of children is not subject to sampling error. The number of low-income children is subject to sampling error.

A separate "time-adjusted" weighting factor was constructed to reflect periods of nonparticipation in the survey. For example, if a member of a reporting unit was ineligible for round three of the survey as a result of institutionalization, foreign residence, or military service, eligibility would commence on the date of return. Similarly, newborns were eligible from their date of birth, while sample members who died were eligible until their date of death. Thus, the "person time-adjusted weight can be thought of as the number of person-years that the sample person represents in the target population" (NCHS, 1983c).

Appendix 3

CONSTRUCTION OF THE
DEPENDENT VARIABLES

The purpose of this appendix is to describe the six dependent variables employed in this study, including measures of the probability and volume of physician visits, as well as the probability of preventive care use. Each measure is differentiated according to office-based physician visits, and physician visits regardless of setting (including services provided by nonphysicians under the supervision of a physician). The construction of the dependent variables is discussed below; Table 27 provides technical documentation on the variable construction.

Aggregate physician visits (variables VSTALLMH and LOGALLMH) include visits to the following categories of providers:

- physicians in office- or clinic-based practice;

- nonphysicians working with a physician in office- or clinic-based practice;

- physicians and nonphysicians in hospital outpatient departments;

- physicians and nonphysicians in emergency rooms; and

- nurse practitioners and physician assistants working independently.

Two categories of visits have been excluded. First, visits to independent providers (except nurse practitioners and physician assistants) have been excluded. Such services reportedly were not provided under physician supervision and, for the purposes of this study, are not considered a physician visit. For example, 193 visits were made to chiropractors and 122

TABLE 27

CONSTRUCTION OF THE DEPENDENT VARIABLES

Variable Name	Brief Description	Variable Construction*
A. Aggregate Physician Visits in 1980		
VSTALLMH	Probability of any physician visit (0,1)	P149 or P152 or P155 or P161 or P164, excluding mental health visits (M155 = 21 or M224 = 15, and M219 NE 4), including visits to independent nurse practitioners and physician assistants (M219 = 4 and M226 = 6 or M226 = 12)
LOGALLMH	Natural log of number of physician visits for children with one or more visits	P149 + P152 + P155 + P161 + P164 minus mental health visits plus independent NP/PA visits, for children with VSTALLMH = 1 (log-transformed)
B. Visits to Private Physicians in 1980		
VSTPRVMH	Probability of visit to physician in private practice (0,1)	P818, excluding mental health visits (M155 = 21 or M224 = 15, and M222 = 1 or M222 = 2, and M219 = 3)
LOGPRVMH	Natural log of number of visits to private physicians for children with one or more visits	P818 minus mental health visits to private physicians, for children with VSTPRVMH = 1 (log transformed)
C. Preventive Care Visits in 1980		
PREVALL	Probability of any preventive visit (0,1)	M155 = 99 and M228 = 2 and M229 = 9 and M230 = 9, and M219 NE 4, except if M226 = 6 or M226 = 12 (NP/PA visits)
PREVPRIV	Probability of preventive visits to private physician (0,1)	M155 = 99 and M228 = 2 and M229 = 9 and M230 = 9 and M222 = 1 or M222 = 2

*The alphanumeric variable label indicates the file and beginning file position for the variable as listed in the NMCUES Public Use Data Tape Documentation (NCHS, 1983c). The file names are referred to as follows: P - Person File and M - Medical Visit File.

to optometrists, and are excluded because these providers did not work under physician supervision, according to the respondent.

Mental health visits, the second category, have been excluded because it is believed that mental health and physical health services have different determinants of utilization. For example, demand for mental health services appears to be more price elastic than demand for other medical care (McGuire, 1981). Mental health visits are defined as visits with the primary condition reported as "mental disorder," or visits to a psychiatrist, psychologist, or social worker.

Physician office visits (variables VSTPRVMH and LOGPRVMH) are defined as visits to physicians in office-based solo or group practice as well as visits to doctors' clinics, excluding mental health visits to such physicians.

Preventive visits (variables PREVALL and PREVPRIV) were required to meet two criteria: (1) the primary reason for visit was a preventive exam and no secondary reason for visit was reported; and (2) no medical condition was reported as causing the visit. The same categories of providers listed above for aggregate visits (VSTALLMH and LOGALLMH) apply to overall preventive care use (PREVALL). However, only those preventive visits provided by a physician in office-based practice have been included in the variable PREVPRIV.

Appendix 4

CONSTRUCTION OF THE INSURANCE COVERAGE MEASURES

This appendix documents the methods used to derive measures of insurance coverage for the descriptive and regression analyses. The public use tape of the National Medical Care Utilization and Expenditure Survey (NMCUES) contains data on six types of third-party coverage: Medicaid, Medicare, private insurance (including prepaid health plans), Civilian Health and Medical Program of the Uniformed Services (CHAMPUS), Indian Health Service (IHS), and "other public" coverage. The tape indicates, for each of the six payment mechanisms, whether the child was insured the entire year, part of the year, or none of the year. In addition, for Medicaid and private insurance, data are provided on whether the child was covered at the midpoint of each quarter in 1980 (i.e., February 15, May 15, August 15, November 15).

The data on health insurance coverage were assembled from several sources, as specified in the NMCUES Public Use Data Tape Documentation (NCHS, 1983c):

1. Coverage as reported in the Health Insurance section of the Questionnaire and verified by the respondent as part of the Summary review process.

2. Coverage as logically imputed when a health insurance plan was indicated as a source of payment in the utilization sections of the Questionnaire and verified by the respondent as part of the Summary review process. For coverage to be logically imputed from utilization data, it had to be indicated as a source of payment more than once during the survey period.

3. Coverage as imputed from Medicare and Medicaid files that related to periods of eligibility.

159

4. Coverage as imputed for periods of missing data by referring to adjacent periods of response, and coverage imputed for periods both preceded and followed by indications of coverage for a particular plan.

Table 28 displays the 46 combinations of insurance coverage among low income children in 1980. The data are unweighted counts of the sample of 1,409 low income children in NMCUES. The majority had one type of coverage for the entire year (721 children, 51.2 percent), or for only part of the year (178 children, 12.6 percent). Of the remainder, 21.9 percent (308 children) were covered by multiple payment mechanisms, while 14.3 percent (202 children) were uninsured during the entire year. None of the low-income children in the sample were covered by Medicare.

The remainder of this section discusses analyses that were conducted and assumptions that were made in an effort to reduce the number of categories of insurance coverage among low income children.

ANALYSIS OF "OTHER PUBLIC" COVERAGE

Of the 308 children with more than one type of coverage, 138 had "other public" coverage in combination with Medicaid, private insurance or CHAMPUS. An additional eight children had "other public" coverage without any other insurance. "Other public" coverage includes payments for care made by the military, the federal government, state and local governments, and public assistance programs (other than Medicaid). (Figure 4 defines each of these types of coverage.)

A dilemma was faced over the classification of children with "other public" coverage, either alone or in combination with another type of insurance. There was a concern that "other public" coverage might not represent a demand-based payment source (comparable to Medicaid or private insurance), but rather a supply-based service delivery mechanism (such as a military facility, community health center, or public health department clinic).

As a result of this concern, a more in-depth investigation was conducted using data not available on the public use tape. The goal was to better understand the patterns of "other public" coverage among low-income children. First, most children covered by CHAMPUS used military facilities or federal government programs (as defined in Figure 4). However, this would be expected based on the provisions of the program (U.S. Department of Defense, 1979).

State and local government sources of payment were most frequently reported in conjunction with Medicaid and private insurance coverage. Based

TABLE 28

INSURANCE COVERAGE OF LOW-INCOME CHILDREN:
ALL REPORTED CATEGORIES*

	Medicaid	Private Insurance	Other Public	CHAMPUS	Indian Health	Frequency	Percent
MEDICAID COVERAGE FULL YEAR							
(3)	Full year	Full year	Full year	---	---	2	0.142
(3)	Full year	Full year	Part year	Part year	---	1	0.071
(3)	Full year	Full year	Part year	---	---	4	0.284
(3)	Full year	Full year	---	Part year	---	1	0.071
(3)	Full year	Full year	---	---	---	23	1.632
(3)	Full year	Part year	Full year	---	---	6	0.426
(3)	Full year	Part year	Part year	---	---	2	0.142
(3)	Full year	Part year	---	Part year	---	1	0.071
(3)	Full year	Part year	---	---	---	45	3.194
(1)	Full year	---	Full year	---	---	7	0.497
(1)	Full year	---	Part year	---	---	34	2.413
(3)	Full year	---	---	Part year	---	1	0.071
(1)	Full year	---	---	---	Full year	3	0.213
(1)	Full year	---	---	---	---	354	25.124
MEDICAID COVERAGE PART YEAR							
(3)	Part year	Full year	Part year	---	---	1	0.071
(3)	Part year	Full year	---	---	---	28	1.987
(3)	Part year	Part year	Part year	---	---	5	0.355
(3)	Part year	Part year	---	---	---	55	3.903
(3)	Part year	---	Full year	Full year	---	1	0.071
(2)	Part year	---	Full year	---	---	2	0.142
(2)	Part year	---	Part year	Full year	---	2	0.142
(2)	Part year	---	Part year	---	---	4	0.284
(2)	Part year	---	---	---	Full year	1	0.071
(2)	Part year	---	---	---	---	74	5.252

TABLE 28 (continued)

INSURANCE COVERAGE OF LOW-INCOME CHILDREN:
ALL-REPORTED CATEGORIES*

	Medicaid	Private Insurance	Other Public	CHAMPUS	Indian Health	Frequency	Percent
NON-MEDICAID COVERAGE							
(4)	---	Full year	Part year	Full year	---	2	0.142
(4)	---	Full year	Part year	---	---	10	0.710
(4)	---	Full year	---	Full year	---	5	0.355
(4)	---	Full year	---	---	---	341	24.202
(4)	---	Part year	Full year	Full year	---	2	0.142
(5)	---	Part year	Full year	Part year	---	3	0.213
(5)	---	Part year	Full year	---	---	2	0.142
(4)	---	Part year	Part year	Full year	---	1	0.071
(5)	---	Part year	Part year	Part year	---	2	0.142
(5)	---	Part year	Part year	---	---	3	0.213
(4)	---	Part year	---	Full year	---	6	0.426
(5)	---	Part year	---	Part year	---	4	0.284
(5)	---	Part year	---	---	---	91	6.458
(4)	---	---	Full year	Full year	---	4	0.284
(6)	---	---	Full year	---	---	1	0.071
(4)	---	---	Part year	Full year	---	27	1.916
(5)	---	---	Part year	Part year	---	8	0.568
(6)	---	---	Part year	---	---	7	0.497
(4)	---	---	---	Full year	---	15	1.065
(5)	---	---	---	Part year	---	6	0.426
(6)	---	---	---	---	Full year	10	0.710
NO COVERAGE IN 1980							
(6)	---	---	---	---	---	202	14.336

*The numeric codes in the first column refer to the analytic categories
displayed in Table 31.

Source: 1980 National Medical Care Utilization and Expenditure Survey.

FIGURE 4

DEFINITION OF TYPES OF "OTHER PUBLIC" COVERAGE

Type of Coverage	NMCUES Coding Scheme
Military	The entry is coded to this category if the entry includes the word Military, Army, Navy, Marine, Air Force, or Coast Guard. If the entry includes both the words U.S. Government and Military, the word Military takes precedence over the words U.S. Government; the entry is coded as Military. Also included in this category are entries indicating direct care, e.g., Military Hospital.
Federal Government	The entry is coded to this category if the entry was reported as U.S. Government or referred to Government without additional specifications. This category includes entries indicating direct care, e.g., Government Clinic.
State/Local Government	The entry is coded to this category if the entry was reported as State, County, or City Government. Excluded from this category are entries identified as Public Assistance. . . An entry is coded as State/Local Government if the entry references only a State or local government . . . If the entry references government and public assistance, public assistance takes precedence.
Public Assistance	The entry is coded to this category if the entry indicates that the source of payment was a form of public assistance and was not coded as Medicaid . . . Public Assistance is coded if words such as Human Health, or Human Services are included in the entry. If the entry references government and public assistance, public assistance takes precedence.

Source: National Center for Health Statistics, Utilization, and Expenditure Survey Branch, National Medical Care Utilization and Expenditure Survey (NMCUES): Health Insurance Plan and Source of Payment Coding Manual, August 6, 1981.

on the guidelines in Figure 4, this form of "other public" coverage includes primarily services provided by state or local public health agencies and community health centers. State and local government programs would not be considered a form of insurance, as such, but rather a service delivery mechanism.

Public assistance (other than Medicaid) was generally reported in conjunction with Medicaid coverage. In fact, all but one of the 43 children with public assistance also had Medicaid coverage. The other child had private insurance part year and "other public" assistance part year.

A supplementary analysis was conducted on the medical visits paid for by "other public" sources. These data support the above conclusion that "other public" coverage tends to be a service delivery mechanism, rather than a form of insurance. Of the 72 visits paid for by public assistance (other than Medicaid), roughly two-thirds were visits to hospital outpatient departments or emergency rooms or to health centers/clinics. All but one of the visits were made by children covered by Medicaid although Medicaid was not reported as a source of payment.

In general, the visits paid for by state or local government sources were made by children covered by Medicaid or private insurance or both. Most of the 112 visits paid for by state or local governments were to health centers or hospital-based facilities. Of the 362 visits paid for by the military, only 19 were made by children not covered by CHAMPUS. Additionally, most of the 21 visits paid for by the federal government were made by children covered by CHAMPUS.

Based on these analysis, "other public" coverage does not appear to be a form of insurance coverage, but rather a service delivery mechanism. Thus, those who only have "other public" coverage are considered uninsured. Where "other public" coverage is combined with another form of third-party coverage (e.g., Medicaid, private health insurance), only the latter type of coverage is considered for the purpose of this study.

CLASSIFICATION OF CHAMPUS
AND IHS COVERAGE

CHAMPUS is a "medical benefits program provided by the Federal Government to help pay for civilian medical care rendered to spouses and children of active duty Uniformed Services personnel, to retired Uniformed Services personnel and their spouses and children, and to spouses and children of deceased active duty and deceased retired personnel." CHAMPUS beneficiaries have the option of obtaining ambulatory care from civilian CHAMPUS-authorized providers, although they are encouraged to obtain medical care from Uniformed Services medical facilities. (Nonemergency inpatient care, however, must be obtained in a Uniformed Services hospital if the beneficiary lives within 40 miles of the facility.) Because ambulatory care is received in civilian and in military facilities, depending on the beneficiary's preference, the CHAMPUS program operates essentially as a private insurance program. Provider participation and reimbursement in CHAMPUS are similar to the Medicare program, with providers electing "assignment" on a case-by-case basis. For the purpose of this study, CHAMPUS coverage is considered a form of private insurance.

The Indian Health Service program, operated by the Federal Government, provides comprehensive health services to about 800,000 Indians and Alaska Natives. Services are provided at 50 IHS hospitals, 101 health centers, and several hundred smaller facilities. In addition, the IHS contracts for services it cannot provide or in areas with no IHS facilities. In fiscal year 1979, 3.3 million outpatient visits were provided by or paid for by the IHS program. Of this number, 1.7 million (51 percent) were visits to IHS hospital clinics; 1.4 million (41 percent) were visits to IHS health centers, satellite clinics, schools, and other units; and 0.3 million (8 percent) were visits to contract physicians (U.S. Department of Health and Human Services, 1980). The IHS program functions primarily as a service delivery mechanism rather than as an insurance mechanism. For the purpose of this study, IHS coverage is not considered a type of insurance coverage. Those with IHS coverage alone are considered uninsured.

ANALYTIC CATEGORIES OF INSURANCE COVERAGE

Based on the preceding analyses, three decisions were made: (1) not to treat "other public" coverage as a separate type of coverage; (2) to treat CHAMPUS as a type of private insurance coverage; and (3) not to treat IHS coverage as an insurance mechanism.

These criteria reduce the number of insurance categories from 46 (Table 28) to 6 (Table 29). The six categories reflect: Medicaid coverage all year and no additional private coverage; Medicaid coverage part year and no other coverage the rest of the year; private insurance (including CHAMPUS) all year; private insurance for only part of the year and no other coverage; both Medicaid and private insurance during the year; and no insurance of any type during 1980.

TABLE 29

INSURANCE COVERAGE OF LOW–INCOME CHILDREN:
ANALYTIC CATEGORIES

Type of Coverage	Number of Low–income Children	Percent of Children
Total	1,409	100.0
Medicaid Coverage	657	46.6
Full year (1)	398	28.2
Part year (2)	81	5.7
With private insurance (3)	178	12.6
Private Insurance		
Full year (4)	435	30.9
Part year (5)	97	6.9
No coverage in 1980 (6)	220	15.6

*The numeric codes in parentheses correspond to the
insurance categories in Table 28.

Source: 1980 National Medical Care Utilization and Expenditure Survey.

Appendix 5

EFFECT OF THE COMPLEX
SAMPLE DESIGN ON
REGRESSION COEFFICIENTS

Table 30 illustrates the effect of the complex sample design on regression coefficients, standard errors, and t-values. Three options are displayed: (1) unweighted estimates with standard errors calculated under simple random sampling (SRS) assumptions; (2) weighted estimates with standard errors calculated under SRS assumptions; and (3) weighted estimates with standard errors adjusted for the complex sample design. The final option takes into account the unequal probabilities of selection, clustering, and stratification. The design effect (option 3, Table 30) is the ratio of the variance calculated under the complex design to the various under SRS.

As discussed in Chapter 3, procedures assuming an SRS design tend to yield a higher number of significant coefficients than would be obtained using procedures that adjust for the complex sample design. Had option 1 been used, all regression coefficients except RATIOGP and RACE3 would have been considered significant at the 0.05 level. Under option 3, however, several other variables are not significant: RSMD, RSNONMD, and PC_MD.

These three variables clearly have important implications for policy. Because Type 1 errors (rejecting a null hypothesis that should be accepted) can be costly to policymakers, the appropriate statistical adjustments should be made to take into account the complex sample design.

TABLE 30

COMPARISON OF REGRESSION COEFFICIENTS UNDER THREE
OPTIONS (Dependent variable is LOGALLMH)

Variable	Regression Coefficient		Standard Error of Coefficient		t-value
UNWEIGHTED SRS DESIGN (OPTION 1)					
REALAGE	-0.117	*	0.016		-7.330
AGESQ	0.006	*	0.001		6.558
RACE3	-0.082		0.052		-1.581
EDSTAT	-0.145	*	0.047		-3.118
CHILDREN	-0.050	*	0.017		-2.912
INCOME	-0.186	E-4*	0.571	E-5	-3.261
OOPPCT	-0.014	*	0.004		-3.724
RSMD	0.155	*	0.070		2.228
RSNONMD	0.149	*	0.074		2.016
PC_MD	-0.0001	*	0.0001		-2.265
RATIOGP	0.031		0.118		-0.267
ERLAND	0.0003	*	0.0001		3.258
PHS_LIM	0.367	*	0.071		5.204
BEDDAYL	0.224	*	0.022		10.098
HOSP	0.401	*	0.077		5.234
WEIGHTED SRS DESIGN (OPTION 2)					
REALAGE	-0.115	*	0.016		-7.335
AGESQ	0.006	*	0.001		6.580
RACE3	-0.069		0.052		-1.338
EDSTAT	-0.169	*	0.047		-3.624
CHILDREN	-0.051	*	0.017		-3.046
INCOME	-0.180	E-4*	0.566	E-5	-3.145
OOPPCT	-0.014	*	0.004		-3.814
RSMD	0.142	*	0.070		2.025
RSNONMD	0.153	*	0.074		2.059
PC_MD	-0.0001	*	0.0006		-2.379
RATIOGP	-0.045		0.118		-0.374
ERLAND	0.0003	*	0.0008		3.610
PHS_LIM	0.401	*	0.071		5.637
BEDDAYL	0.218	*	0.022		9.818
HOSP	0.400	*	0.076		5.278

TABLE 30 (continued)

COMPARISON OF REGRESSION COEFFICIENTS UNDER THREE
OPTIONS (Dependent variable is LOGALLMH)

Variable	Regression Coefficient		Standard Error of Coefficient		t-value	Sq.Rt. of Design Effect
WEIGHTED COMPLEX SAMPLE DESIGN (OPTION 3)						
REALAGE	-0.115	*	0.015		-7.514	0.953
AGESQ	0.006	*	0.001		6.395	1.058
RACE3	-0.069		0.063		-1.095	1.489
EDSTAT	-0.169	*	0.050		-3.365	1.160
CHILDREN	-0.051	*	0.014		-3.619	0.708
INCOME	-0.180	E-4*	0.678	E-5	-2.644	1.416
OOPPCT	-0.014	*	0.003		-4.473	0.727
RSMD	0.142		0.092		1.546	1.717
RSNONMD	0.153		0.101		1.523	1.828
PC_MD	-0.0001		0.0008		-1.709	1.935
RATIOGP	-0.045		0.144		-0.316	1.495
ERLAND	0.0003	*	0.0001		2.791	1.672
PHS_LIM	0.401	*	0.073		5.471	1.062
BEDDAYL	0.218	*	0.022		9.969	0.970
HOSP	0.400	*	0.097		4.140	1.625

*Significant at the 0.05 level.

Source: 1980 National Medical Care Utilization and Expenditure Survey.

LITERATURE CITED

Acton, J.P. Demand for health care among the urban poor, with special emphasis on the role of time. In The role of health insurance in the health services sector. Rosett, R.N., ed. New York: National Bureau of Economic Research, pp. 165-208, 1976.

Aday, L.A. and Andersen, R. Development of indices of access to medical care. Ann Arbor: Health Administration Press, 1975.

Alpert, J.J., Robertson, L.S., Kosa, J., Heagarty, M.C., and Haggerty, R.J. Delivery of health care for children: report of an experiment. Pediatrics 57:917-930, 1976.

Altman, D.E. Health care for the poor. Annals of the American Academy of Political and Social Sciences 468:103-121, 1983.

American Academy of Pediatrics. Committee on Standards of Child Health Care. Standards of child health care, 3rd ed. Evanston, IL: American Academy of Pediatrics, 1977.

Andersen, R. A behavioral model of families' use of health services. Chicago: Center for Health Administration Studies, University of Chicago, 1968.

Andersen, R. Health service distribution and equity. In Equity in health services. Amderson R., Kravitz, J., and Anderson, O., eds. Cambridge, MA: Ballinger Publishing Company, pp. 9-32.

Andersen, R., and Aday, L.A. Access to medical care in the U.S.: realized and potential. Medical Care 16:533-545, 1978.

Andersen, R. and Benham, L. Factors affecting the relationship between family income and medical care consumption. In Empirical studies in health economics. Klarman, H.E., ed. Baltimore: The Johns Hopkins Press, pp. 73-95, 1970.

Andersen, R., Kravitz, J., and Anderson, O.W., eds. Equity in health services: empirical analyses in social policy. Cambridge, MA: Ballinger Publishing Company, 1975.

Andersen, R.M., McCutcheon, A., Aday, L.A., Chiu, G.Y., and Bell, R. Exploring dimensions of access to medical care. Health services research 18:49-74, 1983.

Andersen, R., and Newman, J.F. Societal and individual determinants of medical care utilization in the U.S. Milbank memorial fund quarterly 51:95-124, 1973.

Anderson, J.M. and Thorne, E. Estimates of aggregate personal health care expenditures in 1980--comparison of the National Health Accounts and the National Medical Care Utilization and Expenditure Survey data. Washington, DC: ICF, Inc., mimeo, 1984.

Ashcraft, M.L.F. and Berki, S.E. Health maintenance organizations as Medicaid providers. Annals of the American Academy of Political and Social Sciences 468:122-131, 1983.

Becker, G.S. and Lewis, H.G. On the interaction between the quantity and quality of children. Journal of political economy 81:S279-S288, part 2, 1973.

Berk, M.L., Bernstein, A.B., and Taylor, A.K. The use and availability of medical care in health manpower shortage areas. Inquiry 20:369-380.

Berk, M.L., Wilensky, G.R., and Cohen, S.B. Methodological issues in health surveys: an evaluation of procedures used in the National Medical Care Expenditures Survey. Evaluation review 8:307-326, 1984.

Berki, S.E. and Ashcraft, M.L. On the analysis of ambulatory utilization: an investigation of the roles of need, access and price as predictors of illness and preventive visits. Medical care 17:1163-1181, 1979.

Bice, T.W. and White, K.L. Factors related to the use of health services: an international comparative study. Medical care 7:124-133.

Bonham, G.S. Procedures and questionnaires of the National Medical Care Utilization and Expenditure Survey. Series A, Methodological Report No. 1. DHHS Pub. No. 83-20001. Public Health Service. Washington DC: U.S. Government Printing Office, 1983.

Brewer, W.R. and Freedman, M.A. Causes and implications of variation in hospital utilization. Journal of public health policy 3:445-454, 1982.

Brunswick, A.F. Indicators of health status in adolescence. International journal of health services 6:475-491, 1976.

Bullough, B. The source of ambulatory health services as it relates to preventive care. American journal of public health 64:582-590, 1974.

Children's Defense Fund. EPSDT: Does it spell health care for poor children? Washington, DC: Children's Defense Fund, 1977.

Children's Defense Fund. American children in poverty. Washington, DC: Childrens' Defense Fund, 1984a.

Children's Defense Fund. Deficit Reduction Act of 1984. Washington, DC: Children's Defense Fund, 1984b.

Chiu, G.Y., Aday, L.A., and Andersen, R. An examination of the association of "shortage" and "medical access" indicators. Health policy quarterly 1:142-158, 1981.

Coffey, R.M. The effect of time price on the demand for medical-care services. Journal of human resources 18:407-424, 1983.

Cohen, S.B., and Gridley, G. Present limitations in the availability of statistical packages for the analysis of complex survey data. Paper presented at the annual meeting of the American Statistical Association, 1981.

Cohen, S.B. and Kalsbeek, W.D. Some statistical implications on analysis of the design of the National Medical Care Expenditure Survey. Paper presented at the annual meeting of the American Public Health Association, Los Angeles, California, 1978.

Cohen, S.B. and Kalsbeek, W.D. National Medical Care Expenditure Survey: estimation and sampling variances in the household survey. National Center for Health Services Research, Instruments and Procedures Series No. 2, DHHS Pub. No. (PHS) 81-3281. Washington, DC: U.S. Government Printing Office, 1981.

Colle, A.D. and Grossman, M. Determinants of pediatric care utilization. Journal of human resources 13:115-158 (Suppl.), 1978.

Davidson, S.M. Understanding the growth of emergency room utilization, Medical care 16:122-132, 1978.

Davidson, S.M., Connelly, J.P., Blim, R.D., Strain, J.E., and Taylor, H.D. Consumer cost-sharing as a means to reduce health care costs. Pediatrics 65:168-170, 1980a.

Davidson, S.M., Perloff, J.D., Connelly, J.P., and Schiff, D.W. Pediatricians and Medicaid. Evanston, IL: American Academy of Pediatrics, working paper no 1., 1980b.

Davidson, S.M., Perloff, J.D., Kletke, P.R., Schiff, D.W., and Connelly, J.P. Full and limited Medicaid participation among pediatricians. Pediatrics 72:552-559, 1983.

Davis, K. and Reynolds, R. The impact of Medicare and Medicaid on access to medical care. In The role of health insurance in the health services sector. Rosett, R.N., ed. New York: National Bureau of Economic Research.

Davis, K. and Rowland, D. Uninsured and underserved: inequities in health care in the United States. Milbank memorial fund quarterly 61:149-176, 1983.

Davis K. and Russell, L.B. The substitution of hospital outpatient care for inpatient care. The review of economics and statistics 54:109-120, 1972.

Davis, K. and Schoen, C. Health and the war on poverty: a ten year appraisal. Washington, DC: The Brookings Institution, 1978.

Dutton, D.B. Explaining the low use of health services by the poor: costs, attitudes or delivery systems? American sociological review 43:348-368, 1978.

Dutton, D.B. Patterns of ambulatory health care in five different delivery systems. Medical care 17:221-241, 1979.

Egbonu, L. and Starfield, B. Child health and social status. Pediatrics 69:550-557, 1982.

Eisen, M. Measuring components of children's health status. Medical care 17:902-921, 1979.

Farley, P. Demand elasticities for health care with special emphasis on out-of-pocket price. Division of Intramural Research, National Center for Health Services Research, 1978.

Feldstein, P.J. Health care economics. New York: John Wiley and Sons, 1979.

Fleming, N.S. and Jones, H.C. The impact of outpatient department and emergency room use on costs in the Texas Medicaid program. Medical care 21:892-910, 1983.

Fletcher, R.H., O'Malley, M.S., Fletcher, S.W. Earp, J.L., and Alexander, J.P. Measuring the continuity and coordination of medical care in a system involving multiple providers. Medical care 22:403-411, 1984.

Frieberg, L. Substitution of outpatient care for inpatient care: problems and experience. Journal of health politics, policy, and law 3:479-496, 1979.

Fuchs, V.R. and Kramer, M.J. Determinants of expenditures for physicians' services. DHEW Pub. No. (HSM)73-3013. Washington, DC: U.S. Government Printing Office, 1972.

Fullerton, W.D. Improving private health insurance coverage for children. Paper prepared for the conference on State Action to Improve Child Health, Washington, DC, 1982.

Gabel, J. and Rice, T.H. Reducing public expenditures for physician services: the price of paying less. Journal of health politics, policy, and law 9:595-609, 1985.

Gold, M. The demand for hospital outpatient services. Health services research 19:383-412, 1984.

Gold, M.R. and Rosenberg, R.G. Use of emergency room services by the population of a neighborhood health center. Health services reports 89:65-70, 1974.

Goldman, R. and Grossman, M. The demand for pediatric care: an hedonic approach. Journal of political economy 86:259-280, 1978.

Goldstein, M.S., Siegel, J.M., and Boyer, R. Predicting changes in perceived health status. American journal of public health 74:611-615, 1984.

Gortmaker, S.L. Medicaid and the health care of children in poverty and near poverty: some successes and failures. Medical care 19:567-582, 1981.

Grossman, M. The demand for health: a theoretical and empirical investigation. New York: National Bureau of Economic Research, occasional paper 119, 1972.

Grossman, M., Coate, D., Edwards, L.N., Shakotko, R.A., and Chernichovsky, D. Determinants of children's health. New York: National Bureau of Economic Research, mimeo, 1980.

Hadley, J. Physician participation in Medicaid: evidence from California. Health services research 14:266-280, 1979.

Haggerty, R.J. Roghmann, K.J. and Pless, I.B., eds. Child health and the community. New York: Wiley Publishing Company, 1975.

Health Care Financing Administration. Evaluation options for Medicaid. Report prepared by Urban Systems Research and Engineering and SysteMetrics under contract #HHS-100-81-0026, 1982.

Held, P.J., Manheim, L.M., and Wooldridge, J. Physician acceptance of Medicaid patients. Princeton, NJ: Mathematica Policy Research, mimeo, 1978.

Henderson, M.G. and Hannon, F.L. Cost elements in alternative settings. In Ambulatory care. Altman, S.H., Lion, J., and Williams, J.L., eds. Lexington, MA: D.C. Heath and Company, 1983.

Hennelly, V.D. and Boxerman, S.B. Continuity of medical care: its impact on physician utilization. Medical care 17:1012-1018, 1979.

Hershey, J.C., Luft H.S., and Gianaris, J.M. Making sense out of utilization data. Medical care 13:838-854, 1975.

Hochheiser, L.I., Woodward, K., and Charney, E. Effect of the neighborhood health center on the use of pediatric emergency departments in Rochester, N.Y. New England journal of medicine 285:148-152, 1971.

Holahan, J. Financing health care for the poor: the Medicaid experience. Lexington, MA: Lexington Books, 1975.

Holahan, J. A comparison of Medicaid and Medicare physician reimbursement rates. Washington, DC: The Urban Institute, working paper no. 1306-02-04, 1982a.

Holahan, J. Paying for physicians' services in state Medicaid programs.

Washington, DC: The Urban Institute, working paper no. 2015-00, 1982b.

Holahan, J. The Omnibus Budget Reconciliation Act and Medicaid spending (revised). Unpublished Urban Institute working paper, 1984.

Holahan, J. Paying for physicians' services in state Medicaid programs. Health care financing review 5:99-110, 1984b.

Inman, R.P. The family provision of children's health: an economic analysis. In The role of health insurance in the health services sector. Rosett, R.N. ed. New York: National Bureau of Economic Research, pp. 215-254, 1976.

Intergovernmental Health Policy Project. Recent and proposed changes in state Medicaid programs: A fifty state survey. Washington, DC: George Washington University, 1983.

Intergovernmental Health Policy Project. Primary care case management in Medicaid programs. Focus on... No. 2, 1984.

Jones, S.B. Improving the financing of health care for children and pregnant women. In Better health for our children: a national strategy. The report of the Select Panel for the Promotion of Child Health. Volume IV (Background papers). DHHS (PHS) Pub. No. 79-55071. Washington, DC: U.S. Government Printing Office, 1981.

Kasper, J. Physician utilization and family size. In Equity in health services. Andersen, R., Kravitz, J., and Anderson, O.W., eds. Cambridge, MA: Ballinger Publishing Company, pp. 55-71, 1975.

Kasper, J. The importance of type and usual source of care: physician access by urban and rural low income children. Paper presented at the annual meeting of the American Public Health Association, Dallas, Texas, 1983.

Kelman, H.R., and Lane, D.S. Use of the hospital emergency room in relation to use of private physicians. American journal of public health 66:1189-1191, 1976.

Kleinman, J.C. Medical care use in nonmetropolitan areas. In Health United States, 1981. DHHS Pub. No. (PHS) 82-1232. Washington, DC: U.S. Government Printing Office, pp. 55-61, 1981.

Kleinman, J., Gold, M., and Makuc, D. Use of medical care by the poor: another look at equality. Medical care 19:1011-1030, 1981.

Kovar, M.G. Health status of U.S. children and use of medical care. Public health reports 97:3-15, 1982a.

Kovar, M.G. A methodological study of factors associated with whether children receive adequate medical care. University of North Carolina at Chapel Hill, Institute of Statistics, mimeo series no. 1428, 1982b.

Kovar, M.G. and Meny, D.J. Better health for our children: a national strategy. The report of the Select Panel for the Promotion of Child Health. Volume III (A statistical profile). DHHS (PHS) Pub. No. 79-55071. Washington, DC: U.S. Government Printing Office.

Kronenfeld, J. The Medicaid program and a regular source of care. American journal of public health 68:771-773, 1978a.

Kronenfeld, J. Provider variables and utilization of ambulatory care services. Journal of health and social behavior 19:68-76, 1978b.

Kronenfeld, J. Sources of ambulatory care and utilization models. Health services research 15:3-20, 1980.

Lairson, D.R. and Swint, J.M. A multivariate analysis of the likelihood and volume of preventive visit demand in a prepaid group practice. Medical care 16:730-739, 1978.

Landis, J.R., Lepkowski, J.M., Eklund, S.A., and Stehouwer, S.A. A statistical methodology for analyzing data from a complex survey: the first National Health and Nutrition Examination Survey. National Center for Health Statistics, Series 2, No. 92. DHHS (PHS) Pub. No. 82-1366. Washington, DC: U.S. Government Printing Office, 1982.

Lave, J.R. and Leinhardt, S. The delivery of ambulatory care to the poor: a literature review. Management science 19:P78-P99 (part 2), 1972.

Leopold, E.A. Whom do we reach? A study of health care utilization. Pediatrics 53:341-348, 1974.

Levy, J.C., Bonanno, R.A., Schwartz, C.G., and Sanofsky, P.A. Primary care: patterns of use of pediatric medical facilities. Medical care 17:881-893, 1979.

Lion, J. and Williams, J.L. Medical and socioeconomic case mix in outpatient departments. In Ambulatory care. Altman, S.H., Lion, J., and Williams, J.L. eds. Lexington MA: D.C. Heath and Company, 1983.

Luft, H.S., Hershey, J.C., and Morrell, J. Factors affecting the use of physician services in a rural community. American journal of public health 66:865-871, 1976.

Madans, J. and Kleinman, J. Use of ambulatory care by the poor and nonpoor. In Health, United States, 1980. DHHS Pub. No. (PHS) 81-1232. Washington, DC: U.S. Government Printing Office, 1981.

Manning, W.G., Jr., Newhouse, J.P., Ware, J.E., Jr. The status of health in demand estimation, or beyond excellent, good, fair, and poor. In Economic aspects of health. Fuchs, V., ed. Chicago: University of Chicago Press, pp. 143-184, 1982.

Marcus, A.C. and Stone, J.P. Mode of payment and identification with a regular doctor: a prospective look at reported use of services. Medical care 22:647-657, 1984.

Marquis, M.S. Consumers' knowledge about their health insurance coverage. Health care financing review 5:65-80, 1983.

May, J.J. Utilization of health services and the availability of resources. In Equity in health services. Andersen, R., Kravitz, J., Anderson, O.W., eds. Cambridge, MA: Ballinger Publishing Company, pp. 131-149, 1975.

McGuire, T.G. Financing psychotherapy. Cambridge, MA: Ballinger Publishing Company, 1981.

McKinlay, J.B. and Dutton, D.B. Social-psychological factors affecting health services utilization. In Consumer incentives for health care. Mushkin, S.J., ed. New York: Prodist, pp. 251-303, 1974.

Mechanic, D. Correlates of physician utilization: why do major multivariate studies of physician utilization find trivial psychosocial and organizational effects? Journal of health and social behavior 20:387-396, 1979.

Mitchell, J.B. Medicaid participation by medical and surgical specialists. Medical care 21:929-938, 1983.

Mitchell, J.B. and Schurman, R. Access to OB-GYN services under Medicaid. Chestnut Hill, MA: Center for Health Economics Research, mimeo, 1982.

Moser, B., Whitmore, R., Frick, G.G., Lucas, R., Smith, P., and Brown, B. Public use family data tape documentation. National Medical Care Utilization and Expenditure Survey, 1980. Prepared for National Center for Health Statistics and Health Care Financing Administration. RTI Project No. 251U-1898-H, 1984.

Mugge, R.H. Persons receiving care from selected health care practitioners, United States, 1980. National Medical Care Utilization and Expenditure Survey. Series B, Descriptive Report No. 6. DHHS Pub. No. 84-20206. National Center for Health Statistics, Public Health Service, Washington, DC: U.S. Government Printing Office, 1984.

Muse, D.N. and Sawyer, D. The Medicare and Medicaid data book, 1981. Health care financing program statistics. DHHS (HCFA) Pub. No. 03128. Washington, DC: U.S. Government Printing Office, 1982.

National Center for Health Statistics. Physician visits, volume and interval since last visit, United States, 1980. Series 10, No. 144. DHHS (PHS) Pub. No. 83-1572. Washington, DC: U.S. Government Printing Office, 1983a.

National Center for Health Statistics. Patterns of ambulatory care in pediatrics: The National Ambulatory Medical Care Survey, United States, January 1980-December 1981. Series 13, No. 75. DHHS (PHS) Pub. No. 84-1736. Washington, DC: U.S. Government Printing Office, 1983b.

National Center for Health Statistics. Public use data tape documentation: National Medical Care Utilization and Expenditure Survey, 1980. Washington, DC: U.S. Government Printing Office, 1983c.

National Center for Health Statistics. Utilization and Expenditure Survey Branch. NMCUES health insurance plan and source of payment coding manual, mimeo, 1981.

Office of Data Analysis and Management (ODAM). Technical documentation with field length and alpha/numeric indicators for the Area Resource File (ARF). Rockville, MD: Bureau of Health Professions, 1984.

Okada, L.M., and Wan, T.T.H. Impact of community health centers and Medicaid on the use of health services. Public health reports 95:520-534, 1980.

Orr, S.T. and Miller, C.A. Utilization of health services by poor children since the advent of Medicaid. Medical care 19:583-590, 1981.

Paringer, L. The impact of state Medicaid policy on expenditures and utilization of hospital and ambulatory services. Paper presented at the annual meeting of the American Public Health Association, Anaheim, CA, 1984.

Pindyck, R.S. and Rubinfeld, D.L. Econometric models and economic forecasts, 2nd ed. New York: McGraw-Hill Book Company, 1981.

Pope, C.R., Yoshioka, S.S., and Greenlick, M.R. Determinants of medical care utilization: the use of the telephone for reporting symptoms. Journal of health and social behavior 12:155-162, 1971.

President's Commission for the Study of Ethical Problems in Medicine and Biomedical and Behavioral Research. Securing access to health care. Volume one: report. Washington, DC: U.S. Government Printing Office, 1983.

Rice, T. Determinants of physician assignment rates by the type of service. Health care financing review 5:33-42, 1984.

Robert Wood Johnson Foundation. Updated report on access to health care for the American people. Princeton, NJ: The Robert Wood Johnson Foundation, 1983.

Roghmann, K.J. The utilization of health services: ambulatory care--decreasing utilization rates. In Child health and the community. Haggerty, R. J., Roghmann, K.J., Pless, M.B. eds. New York: Wiley, pp. 169-177, 1975.

Roghmann, K.J. and Haggerty, R.J. Daily stress, illness and use of health services in young families. Pediatric research 7:520-526, 1973.

Roghmann, K.J., Haggerty, R.J., and Lorenz, R. Anticipated and actual effects of Medicaid on the medical-care pattern of children. New England journal of medicine 285:1053-1057, 1971.

Rosenblatt, D. and Suchman, E.A. The underutilization of medical care services by blue-collarites. In Blue collar world. Englewood Cliffs, NJ: Prentice-Hall, 1964.

Rosenbaltt, R.A. and Moscovice, I.S. The physician as gatekeeper: determinants of physicians' hospitalization rates. Medical care 22:150-159, 1984.

Rosenstock, I.M. Why people use health services. Milbank memorial fund quarterly 44:94-127 (part 2), 1966.

Rossiter, L.F. and Wilensky, G.R. A reexamination of the use of physician services: the role of physician-initiated demand. Inquiry 20:162-172, 1983.

Rundall, T.G. and Wheeler, J.R.C. The effect of income on use of preventive care: an evaluation of alternative explanations. Journal of health and social behavior 20:397-406, 1979.

Rymer, M.P., Oksman, C.G., Bailis, L.N., and Ellwood, D.T. Medicaid eligibility: problems and solutions. Boulder, CO: Westview Press, 1979.

Salber, E.J. Feldman, J.J., Rosenberg, L.A., and Williams, S. Utilization of services at a neighborhood health center. Pediatrics 47:415-423, 1971.

Salkever, D.S. Accessibility and the demand for preventive care. Social science and medicine 10:469-475, 1976.

Sawyer, D., Ruther, M., Pagan-Berlucchi, A., and Muse, D.N. The Medicare and Medicaid data book, 1983. Baltimore, MD: Health Care Financing Administration, HCFA Pub. No. 03156, 1983.

Scherzer, L.N., Druckman, R., and Alpert, J.J. Care-seeking patterns of families using a municipal hospital emergency room. Medical care 18:289-296, 1980.

Select Panel for the Promotion of Child Health. Better health for our children: a national strategy, Volume II (Analysis and recommendations for selected federal programs). DHHS (PHS) Pub. No. 79-55071. Washington, DC: U.S. Government Printing Office, 1981.

Shadish, W. Effectiveness of preventive child health care. Baltimore, MD: Health Care Finanancing Administration, Office of Research, Demonstrations, and Statistics, 1981.

Shah, B.V. SESUDAAN: standard errors program for computing of standardized rates from sample survey data. Research Triangle Park, NC: Research Triangle Institute, 1981.

Shah, B.V. SURREGR: standard errors of regression coefficients from sample survey data. Research Triangle Park, NC: Research Triangle Insitute, 1982.

Sharp, K., Ross, C.E., and Cockerham, W.C. Symptoms, beliefs, and the use of physician services among the disadvantaged. Journal of health and social behavior 24:255-263, 1983.

Skinner, E.A., German, P.S., Shapiro, S., Chase, G.A., and Zalber, A.G. Use of ambulatory health services by the near poor. American journal of public health 68:1195-1201, 1978.

Slesinger, D.P. The utilization of preventive medical services by urban black mothers. In The growth of bureaucratic medicine. Mechanic, D., ed. New York: Wiley, 1976.

Sloan, F., Mitchell, J.B., and Cromwell, J. Physician participation in state Medicaid programs. Journal of human resources 13:211-245 (suppl.), 1978.

Sloan, F.A. and Steinwald, B. Physician participation in health insurance plans: evidence on Blue Shield. The journal of human resources 13:237-263, 1978.

Smythe-Staruch, K., Breslau, N., Weitzman, M., and Gortmaker, S. Use of health services by chronically ill and disabled children. Medical care 22:310-328, 1984.

Spitz, B. Contracting with health maintenance organizations. In New approaches to the Medicaid crisis. Blendon, R.J. and Moloney, T.W., eds. New York: F and S Press, 1982.

Stevens, R. and Stevens, R. Welfare medicine in America: a case study of Medicaid. New York: The Free Press, 1974.

Suchman, E. Social patterns of illness and medical care. Journal of health and human behavior 6:2-16, 1965.

Tanner, J.L., Cockerham, W.C., and Spaeth, J.L. Predicting physician utilization. Medical care 21:360-369, 1983.

Taube, C.A., Kessler, L., and Burns, B. Estimating the probability and level of ambulatory mental health use, unpublished paper, 1984.

Tessler, R. Birth order, family size, and children's use of health services. Health services research 15:55-62, 1980.

Tessler, R. and Mechanic, D. Factors affecting children's use of physician services in prepaid group practice. Medical care 16:33-46.

Tryon, A.F., Powell, E., and Roghmann, K. Anticipated health behavior of families in relation to Medicaid. Public health reports 85:1021-1028, 1970.

U.S. Congress, Congressional Budget Office. Health differentials between white and non-white Americans. Washington, DC: Congress of the United States, Congressional Budget Office, 1977.

U.S. Congress, Congressional Budget Office. Medicaid: choices for 1982 and beyond. Washington, DC: Congress of the United States, Congressional Budget Office, 1982.

U.S. Congress, House, Committee on Energy and Commerce. Health budget proposals. Hearings before a subcommittee of the House Committee on Energy and Commerce on Medicaid maternal and child health initiatives, 98th Cong., 1st sess., 1983.

U.S. Department of Commerce. Characteristics of the population below the poverty level: 1981. Current Population Reports, series P-60, no. 138, 1983a.

U.S. Department of Commerce. Statistical abstract of the United States: 1984 (104th edition). Washington, DC: U.S. Government Printing Office, 1983b.

U.S. Department of Defense. CHAMPUS handbook. Washington, DC: U.S. Government Printing Office, 1979.

U.S. Department of Health and Human Services. The Indian health program of the U.S. Public Health Service. Rockville, MD: U.S. Department of Health and Human Services, DHHS Pub. No. (HSA) 80-1003, 1980.

U.S. General Accounting Office. Comptroller General of the U.S. Outpatient health care in inner cities: its users, services and problems. Pub. No. MWD-75-81, 1975.

Valdez, R.B., Rogers, W.H., Ware, J.E., Keeler, E.B., Donald, C.A., Lohr, K.M., Goldberg, G.A., Masthay, P.C., Newhouse, J.P., and Brook, R.H. Rand health insurance study: the consequences of cost sharing for children's health. Paper presented at the annual meeting of the American Public Health Association, Anaheim, CA, 1984.

Wan, T.T.H. and Gray, L.C. Differential access to preventive services for young children in low-income urban areas. Journal of health and social behavior 19:312-324, 1978.

Wan, T.T.H. and Soifer, S.J. Determinants of physician utilization: a causal analysis. Journal of health and social behavior 15:100-108, 1974.

Wilensky, G.R. and Berk M.L. Health care, the poor, and the role of Medicaid. Health affairs 1:93-100, 1982.

Wilensky, G.R. and Walden, DC Minorities, poverty, and the uninsured. Paper presented at the annual meeting of the American Public Health Association, Los Angeles, CA, 1981.

Wilensky, G.R., Walden, D.C., and Kasper, J.A. The uninsured and their use of health services. Paper presented at the annual meeting of the American Statistical Association, 1981.

Williams, A.P., Schwartz, W.B., Newhouse, J.P., and Bennett, B.W. How many miles to the doctor? New England journal of medicine 309:958-963, 1983.

Wilson, R. Do health indicators indicate health? American journal of public health 71:461-463, 1981.

Wilson, R. and White, E.L. Changes in mordibity, disability, and utilization differentials between the poor and the nonpoor: data from the Health Interview Survey, 1964 and 1973. Medical care 15:636-646, 1977.

Wolfe, B.L. Children's utilization of medical care. Medical care 18:1196-1207, 1980.

Wolinsky, F.D. Assessing the effects of predisposing, enabling, and illness-morbidity characteristics on health service utilization. Journal of health and social behavior 19:384-396, 1978.

Zola, I.K. Illness behavior of the working class: implications and recommendations. In Blue collar world. Englewood Cliffs, NJ: Prentice-Hall, 1964.